# THE INCREDIBLE WORLD OF NICHIREN BUDDHISM

*Suraj Jagtiani*

authorHOUSE®

*AuthorHouse™ UK Ltd.*
*500 Avebury Boulevard*
*Central Milton Keynes, MK9 2BE*
*www.authorhouse.co.uk*
*Phone: 08001974150*

*The views and interpretations expressed in this book are those solely of the author.*

*©2011. Suraj Jagtiani. All rights reserved.*

*No part of this book may be reproduced, stored in a retrieval system, or transmitted by any means without the written permission of the author.*

*First published by AuthorHouse 03/19/2011*

*ISBN: 978-1-4520-4234-3*

*This book is printed on acid-free paper.*

THE LIFE OF ALL BUDDHAS, PAST, PRESENT
AND FUTURE FLOWS THROUGH EACH OF
OUR LIVES.

# CONTENTS

| | |
|---|---:|
| Foreword | ix |

## **GENERAL OVERVIEW** — 1

| | |
|---|---:|
| WHAT IS BUDDHISM | 2 |
| BASICS OF NICHIREN BUDDHISM | 4 |
| RELATIONSHIP BETWEEN BUDDHISM AND OTHER BELIEFS, RELIGIONS & SCIENCE | 6 |
| SHAKYAMUNI | 9 |
| NICHIREN DAISHONIN | 11 |
| HISTORY | 14 |
|   1. Teachings of Shakyamuni | 14 |
|   2. Spread of Buddhism | 15 |
|   3. Mahayana & Hinayana Buddhism | 16 |
|   4. Notable Buddhist Scholars | 19 |
|   5. Three Stages of propagation – Former/middle/latter days | 19 |
|   6. Buddhism in India | 20 |
|   7. Buddhism in China | 20 |
|   8. Buddhism in Japan | 22 |
|   9. Buddhist sects in Japan | 23 |

| | |
|---|---|
| 10. Nichiren Soshu (Orthodox Nichiren sect) | 24 |
| 11. Soka Gakkai | 24 |

# NICHIREN BUDDHISM     27

## A). GENERAL CONCEPTS     28

| | |
|---|---|
| 1. The Need for Religious Philosophy | 28 |
| 2. Faith, Benefit, Happiness | 28 |
| 3. The law of Causation (Cause & Effect) | 30 |
| 4. Buddhahood | 34 |

## B). BUDDHIST DOCTRINE     36

| | |
|---|---|
| 1. The Law | 36 |
| 2. Ichinen Sanzen | 37 |
| 3. The Ten Worlds | 39 |
| 4. Mutual Possession of the Ten Worlds | 43 |
| 5. The Ten Factors of Life | 43 |
| 6. The Three Realms of Existence | 46 |
| 7. The Three Truths | 47 |
| 8. Karma | 49 |
| 9. Eternity of Life | 53 |
| 10. Nine Levels of Consciousness | 54 |
| 11. The Reality of Life | 55 |
| 12. General | 56 |
|    a. Reality & Wisdom | 56 |
|    b. Three Powerful Enemies | 56 |
|    c. The Three Virtues | 57 |
|    d. The Three Treasures | 58 |
|    e. The Three Proofs | 58 |

## C). LOTUS SUTRA     60

| | |
|---|---|
| 1. Brief Overview | 60 |
| 2. Hoben & Juryo Chapters | 67 |
| 3. The Three Expedients | 72 |

| | |
|---|---|
| D). CHAPTERS OF THE LOTUS SUTRA | 73 |
| E). PRACTICE | 76 |
| 1. Faith, Practice & Study | 76 |
| 2. Nam Myoho Renge Kyo | 80 |
| 3. The Three Great Secret Laws | 84 |
| 4. Five Guides for Propagation | 86 |
| 5. Kosen Rofu | 87 |
| 6. Supreme Goal of Life | 88 |
| 7. Benefits | 89 |
| 8. General | 91 |
| a. Oneness of Person & The Law | 91 |
| b. Oneness of Body & Mind / Life & its Environment / Being & Essence | 91 |
| c. Chanting / Meditation / Positive Thinking | 93 |
| F). GENERAL IDEAS, THOUGHTS & TEACHINGS | 94 |
| G). EXTENDED GLOSSARY | 97 |
| 1. Anut Tara Samyak Sambodhi | 97 |
| 2. Arhat | 97 |
| 3. Bodhisattva | 97 |
| 4. Buddha Nature | 98 |
| 5. Compassion | 99 |
| 6. The Concept of Soku | 99 |
| 7. Dharma | 99 |
| 8. The Entity of Life | 100 |
| 9. Eye Opening Ceremony | 100 |
| 10. Fivefold Comparison | 100 |
| 11. The Five Components | 101 |
| 12. The Five Skandas | 102 |
| 13. The Four Noble Truths / Paths | 102 |
| 14. The Fourteen Slanders | 102 |
| 15. The Eightfold Noble Paths | 103 |
| 16. Gohonzon | 103 |
| 17. Gosho | 105 |
| 18. The High Sanctuary | 106 |
| 19. Human Revolution | 106 |

20. Impermanence — 107
21. Jigage — 107
22. Kuon Ganjo — 107
23. Life & Death — 108
24. Note on the Parable of the Skilled Physician & his Sick Children — 109
25. Principal of Causality — 111
26. Rebirth — 112
27. Rissho Ankoku Ron — 112
28. Samsara — 113
29. The Six Paramitas — 113
30. Soka Kyoiki Gakkai — 114
31. Three Aspects of Life — 115
32. The Three Calamities & Seven Disasters — 115
33. The Three Enlightened Bodies — 116
34. The Three Obstacles & Four Devils — 116
35. The Three Vehicles — 117
36. The Thirty Four Negatives — 118
37. True & Provisional Buddhas, — 119
38. Yuga / Kalpa — 120

## **CONCLUSION** — 121

## **ACKNOWLEDGEMENTS** — 122

# **FOREWORD**

Recently there has been a marked shift in human attitudes, from basic traditional values towards raw & impersonal materialistic values. This has led to more competitive living environments, self centered needs & wants, which have inevitably and generally led to more failures, disappointments, let downs and a general feeling of apathy – and ultimately unhappiness.

It is in these trying times of depression and unhappiness that one tends to show a marked increase in one's spiritual values. Initially this is more so as an expedient, to lead one to happiness.

This is where the role that religious philosophy plays in our lives is of crucial importance. Rather than act as a crutch – providing support in our time of need – a philosophy has to be more meaningful, thus being more than just a transient phase in one's life.

The advent of modern technologies, improved rapid communication & heightened awareness, has resulted in the establishment of numerous "new age" religions, philosophies and beliefs. Unfortunately most of these are focused on self gain and how to trick gullible unsuspecting people out of their hard earned money.

Most people are already introduced to religion

at an early age, through family and the various doctrines & ideologies prevalent in the indigenous cultures of their countries. In order for a religion to be effective, one must be able to identify their own thoughts & attitudes with the doctrine, so as to help develop the self improvement of our values & compassion. This leads to our working towards the betterment of society, pursuit of the truth & above all lead us towards a meaningful & happy life.

Religion is personal. There are many religions & philosophies, from the established ones to the various newer schools of thought. Most have good, decent, logical ideologies & each one of us must individually decide on the choice of religion, which is again based on one's circumstances, exposure, understanding, upbringing & society. It would be improper to classify one religion as good or bad as there are many aspects to any religion depending upon one's viewpoint.

I can only comment personally, on my introduction to the religion and philosophy of Nichiren Daishonin's Buddhism.

My wife, Raju, was first introduced to Nichiren Buddhism nearly 20 years ago and ever since then, I have always had a peripheral interaction with this philosophy. Over the years Raju progressed further within the SGI which led to my further exposure and understanding of Nichiren Buddhism.

Albeit, at first I would listen to Raju extolling the vast and immense benefits that accrue from chanting "Nam Myoho Renge Kyo", to briefly scanning some magazines and books and also chanting with her when she insisted. However these were obliging actions without a clear knowledge and understanding of the faith.

Whilst I was a passive supporter and never objected to Raju's faith (not that I would have had a say anyway), I never wholeheartedly got involved into Nichiren Buddhism. I used to peruse books on general Buddhism, and at times got very confused as to the various streams, sects, sub sects and precepts that all stemmed from this unique faith that was expounded by Shakyamuni, nearly 2600 years ago. Even whilst reading on Nichiren Buddhism, my concentration was not at its sharpest, resulting in my not perceiving correctly what was read. Lack of time (or rather my not making a sincere effort), led to passive acceptance with the age old adage of "it can't hurt anyway".

It was during an unfortunate period in my life that I began to reflect on what went wrong & why. Being denied the basic, taken for granted things in life led to the "opening of my eyes" & made me reflect more on the course of my life henceforth. Reading on Nichiren Buddhism in detail & with concentration, there was a lot I could identify with, that also had an element of commonsense & logic, which was very important to me.

Some of the reading material I had access to, I found either too brief or too detailed. I started to assimilate copious notes on this philosophy. The more I read, the more I began to understand and learn, identifying with Nichiren Buddhism with a zeal and interest I did not think possible. This led me to make a vow that I would, one day, publish an easy to read guide, which would be of interest to anyone wanting to seek further information on the philosophy of Nichiren Buddhism.

Basically, having faith in the teachings gave me the confidence to overcome my negative position & my practice of gongyo, chanting & "study", led to my acceptance of my situation without any bitterness. I have begun to, never to take things for granted, seek happiness & fulfillment from within, be more considerate & caring of others and cherish & protect the welfare & happiness of my family. Chanting in itself has an overpowering soothing effect, which somehow brings things into sharper focus & clarity. I am in charge of my present & future and it is up to me to dictate the destiny of the course of my life. This has led to my having an unwavering faith & belief.

The culmination of my unstinting faith and belief led to a sudden and inexplicable return to the folds of my family, which has forever transformed even my slightest doubts, as I have seen actual proof of my faith.

I hope this book will be a useful guide to all those who wish to know more and understand the wonderful philosophy of Nichiren Buddhism.

In conclusion, I say to all my fellow Buddhists – Having faith and belief is one thing, but truly understanding and comprehending, even, the basics of Nichiren Buddhism, and acting thereon, will unleash the strength and power of Nam Myoho Renge Kyo from within you, which in turn will ameliorate your current state of life. I promise.

I close with the apt words of Daisaku Ikeda

– "Society is complex & harsh, demanding that you struggle hard to survive. No one can make you happy. Everything depends on you as to whether or not you attain happiness – A human being is destined to a life of great suffering if he is weak & vulnerable to his external surroundings."

# GENERAL OVERVIEW

"NOW, NO MATTER WHAT, STRIVE IN FAITH AND BE KNOWN AS A VOTARY OF THE LOTUS SUTRA, AND REMAIN MY DISCIPLE FOR THE REST OF YOUR LIFE. IF YOU ARE OF THE SAME MIND AS NICHIREN, YOU MUST BE A BODHISATTVA OF THE EARTH. AND IF YOU ARE A BODHISATTVA OF THE EARTH, THERE IS NOT THE SLIGHTEST DOUBT THAT YOU HAVE BEEN A DISCIPLE OF SHAKYAMUNI BUDDHA FROM THE REMOTE PAST." (WND, 385)

# WHAT IS BUDDHISM

Buddhism is a philosophy of life concerned with the essential nature of humanity. Buddhism is the name given to the teachings (sutras) that were expounded by Shakyamuni Buddha. Buddhism works to awaken people to the ultimate reality of life, lying below impulses & desires so that they can consciously maintain balance in their lives. Its teachings enable people to attain enlightenment and become Buddhas themselves. Buddha means the Enlightened One and in a sense means that a Buddha is one who realizes in his inherent self, the reality of life. Buddhists perceive the ultimate reality of life equally within all human beings, and accordingly strive to awaken others to the dignity of their own lives.

Buddhism is reason (WND, 389) and its concepts do not contradict common sense. Its teachings are essentially pragmatic. The highest teachings of Buddhism show that the desire for overcoming sufferings can be regarded as one of the biggest incentives for inner transformation, self development, compassion & progress. The true spirit of Buddhism has always been concerned with providing practical solutions to the problems of suffering rather than debating the various aspects of its philosophy.

People have a habit of wanting to rely on somebody. Even if that somebody were the Buddha, he is still someone other than oneself. Buddhism is not about believing in the Buddha. His teachings are the path for us to live as ourselves. So, Buddhism is not just the teachings of the Buddha, it is the path for us to actualize our own selves in becoming Buddhas. That is why it is not Buddha that we are to depend upon, but only our own selves and the truth. In this way, Buddhism is a religion of self – investigation.

A Buddha is a person who has developed introspective wisdom into the depths of his life & discovered the eternal truth therein. Shakyamuni & his disciples explained the Law from various angles & gave it a systematic philosophical basis. This led to the establishment of Buddhism as a religion.

In the latter years of his life, Shakyamuni revealed his most profound teaching, the Lotus Sutra and urged his disciples to focus on this teaching and that all other sutras were preparatory. Shakyamuni predicted that at "the beginning of the Latter Day of the Law", a Buddha would appear who would reveal the correct teaching based on his highest teaching, the Lotus Sutra. Nichiren Daishonin declared that the Lotus Sutra is supreme amongst all the Buddhist teachings mainly because that it teaches that everyone has Buddhahood inherent within them and the eternity of life

It is probably the easily grasped, practical & down to earth nature of these teachings that has caused the rapid and far reaching spread of Nichiren Buddhism in recent times.

"To think of Buddhism as a placid teaching expounded in a bucolic setting under the shade of a tree is a totally false image. Buddhism is intensely practical, not escapist. It lives in human society and has been handed down among the

people – this is the true flow of Buddhism."
Daisaku Ikeda

## BASICS OF NICHIREN BUDDHISM

Nichiren Buddhism is evolved from Mahayana Buddhism. The basis of this Buddhism is "Nam Myoho Renge Kyo" which encompasses the entire teachings of the 28 chapter LOTUS SUTRA. It is a philosophy that teaches that everyone can attain enlightenment and Buddhahood in this lifetime by having faith in the 'Mystic Law' of Nam Myoho Renge Kyo. It entails the practice of gongyo & chanting daimoku, having sincere faith in the 'Mystic Law' (Gohonzon), & study of the Buddhist teachings (scriptures), and above all putting into action what we have learnt, in our daily lives.

In Nichiren Buddhism, the Lotus Sutra, as expounded by Shakyamuni, is the teaching that is judged supreme as it enables all people, good or evil, to attain Buddhahood. Prayer takes the form of chanting Nam Myoho Renge Kyo, which reveals one's inherent Buddhahood.

The twice daily practice of performing gongyo & chanting Nam Myoho Renge Kyo, in front of the Gohonzon is an integral part in the practice of this Buddhism. Central to the Buddhist teachings is the 'Law of Cause & Effect'. Positive causes are attained by chanting Nam Myoho Renge Kyo & striving to affect a human revolution within our lives. The practice of 'Kosen Rofu' is an essential part of Nichiren Daishonin's Buddhism.

Belief in the Gohonzon, chanting daimoku and

spreading the teachings will certainly lead to enlightenment. Nichiren Daishonin clearly explained the ultimate reality of life, the 'Mystic Law' which is Nam Myoho Renge Kyo.

Faith in the Gohonzon enables one to draw forth the essential reality of Nam Myoho Renge Kyo (the Buddha nature), which has been inherent in our lives since time beginning. Nichiren Daishonin has opened the portals, of attaining Buddhahood, to all people.

In Nichiren Buddhism, the truth of Nam Myoho Renge Kyo and the Gohonzon took over 2000 years of Buddhist thinking and practice to crystallize into its essential form. Buddhists do not believe in the 'afterlife' but rather in the eternity of life. In Buddhism the material & spiritual are of equal importance. It enables one to throw away all crutches & props to stand alone as fulfilled, wise, compassionate and creative human beings, living life to the full and creating value out of every situation, even seemingly hopeless ones. The Buddhism of Nichiren Daishonin is rooted in daily life, and, as such, does not provide a spiritual panacea, but a practical system of thought, word & deed, with direct relevance to the lives of all who practice it. This is achieved by bringing out their inherent Buddhahood, by chanting Nam Myoho Renge Kyo to the Gohonzon. Nichiren Buddhism also teaches us "The Art of Living", which is how to fundamentally improve the quality of our lives & that of others so that we may truly become fulfilled and happy in this lifetime. This value creating doctrine of Nichiren Buddhism brings out the inherent strength and wisdom which everyone possesses within themselves – their Buddhahood – by chanting Nam Myoho Renge Kyo. As Nichiren Daishon states "In Buddhism, that teaching is supreme which enables all people, whether good or evil, to become Buddhas. So reasonable a standard, can surely be grasped by anyone." Nichiren Daishonin's Buddhism teaches that nothing bests actual proof. In this regard it stands alone among the religions of the world.

## RELATIONSHIP BETWEEN BUDDHISM AND OTHER BELIEFS, RELIGIONS & SCIENCE

Like scientific laws, the principles of Nichiren Buddhism transcend time and place.
In ancient times the forces of nature were regarded as a transcendental being or God. Natural calamities were often regarded as the work of God's anger. This led to the formation of the belief that it was God's will that created the universe & all beings within it. Ancient religions regarded natural social phenomena as manifestations of God's will & wisdom.
Buddhahood is the ultimate goal for a man to attain. Whereas in Christianity, man can never become God completely, in Buddhism man can become a Buddha. Buddhism does not deny the existence of God per se. It describes Gods as beneficial forces innate in social & natural surroundings which work to protect us. Some early Christian sects, specially the Gnostics,

identify Jesus as an embodiment of a Supreme Being (akin to an enlightened Buddha) who became incarnate to bring Gnosis – esoteric knowledge which transcends time and deemed as necessary to attaining salvation / enlightenment – to this Earth.

Christianity expounds the ideal of love for all mankind, especially for the less fortunate & unhappy. Some modern Christian theologians interpret God as a Law, immaterial & universal, which influences phenomena throughout the universe. These views have more in common with Buddhist philosophies & the fact that it developed at all indicates an underlying deep connection between the two streams of thought. Even in its teachings there are marked similarities between the two religions. For instance, the kingdom of God (in Christianity) is startlingly similar to the 'Perfect Land of Pure Bliss' (as expounded in early provisional Mahayana teachings). Also, Christian teachings & commandments seem to equally describe the way of a Bodhisattva.

Some early Christian writers record exchanges between themselves and religious missions from India. Such exchanges, many more of which have gone unrecorded, suggest that Buddhism may have had some influence on early Christianity. As stated by Bentley in "Old World Encounters" – "Scholars have often considered the possibility that Buddhism influenced the early development of Christianity."

Science investigates the phenomenal world in which we live & act, dealing with the objectively perceptible aspects of existence, including the physical & material aspects of all phenomena.

In Buddhism, Ke is called temporary existence. As postulated in Buddhist philosophy, all things from the smallest sub atomic particle to the universe undergoes the cycle of birth & death. Scientific theory states that the universe itself was born with the 'Big Bang' – an explosion of "something". The universe is expanding and will continue to do so ad infinitum. It is speculative whether this expansion will cease or begin to contract, possibly to expand again at some later date. Buddhist perception is that the universe will follow the continuous rhythm of Myoho. Certainly, it is seen that stars and other celestial bodies are born & die continuously.

All things are undergoing constant change. Buddhism regards all existence as temporary, as whatever exists at any one moment, no longer exists in the same form or situation in the next. This realization is however, not only the preserve of Buddhism but is supported by discoveries made by pioneers of quantum physics as well. It is with looking at them to see how close they approach the teachings of Buddhism about the physical world.

Scientific research & experiments have bought scientists closer to the truth of non-substantiality, where even the smallest particle 'exists' but defies all attempts to define the basis of its existence. As one of the great scientific minds once said – "Theoretical physics is actual philosophy".

The realms of science are widening, but still has limitations as 'scientific approach' is based on methodical, objective observation & reasoning, which lead to some realms being outside the reach of scientific cognition. Such realms can be grasped, if at all, by the subjective & intuitive mind. In its search for the truth, science draws on mainly analytical & inductive reasoning, while Buddhist reasoning is a comprehensive method of deduction & intuition. Science plays a powerful role in objective cognition, but how effectively we use this method to improve our lives is decided by the degree to which we are awakened to the truth in the depths of our lives. Science & Buddhism are truly complimentary to each other.

"Religion without science is blind; science without religion is lame."- Albert Einstein

## SHAKYAMUNI

Shakyamuni is known as Buddha – "The Enlightened One". He is often referred to as the leader of the "greatest office in the spiritual hierarchy of mankind." He realized the ultimate reality of life, and his teachings have collectively come to be called Buddhism.

Shakyamuni was born a prince, Siddhartha Gautama, the son of King Shuddhodana. He lived in his kingdom for nearly 25 years, sheltered from the unpleasant realities of all human suffering. He eventually encountered them in the form of a sick person, an old senile person, a corpse & a religious ascetic. These experiences affected him profoundly. Realizing that his way of life leads only to death and no real lasting value,

Prince Siddhartha decided to leave his home and try to understand the conflicts and emotions he was going through. He practiced the extreme austerities & teachings of various religious sects of his day, but rejected them as incapable of providing the answer that he sought. He went into the forest to meditate under a Pipal tree and in time entered into a state of profound meditation & as a result became enlightened to the true nature of life.

Siddhartha dwelt at Sravasti, in the Jeta grove, in the garden of Anathapindaka, together with a large company of Bhikus (Frairs) – including Elders, Disciples, Arhats such as Shariputra & Mahakakasyapa, noble minded Bodhisattvas such as Manjusri & B.Ajita, with Sakra (The Indra or king of Devas) and with Brahmin Sahampati.

After many years of persistent, single minded effort, meeting & overcoming one difficulty after another, he attained enlightenment. Having, thus, freed himself from all delusions & suffering, he aspired to help others to reach enlightenment too; his compassion was limitless. He spent the remaining years of his life sharing and expounding the path to enlightenment.

His teachings were fluid & varied according to the needs, capabilities & personalities of his students & followers. He led them skillfully towards the understanding of the ultimate reality of life. His teachings were recorded in the various Sutras, most of which were preparatory for the core of his teachings – The Lotus Sutra. He encouraged his disciples to turn inwards towards their own "life" instead of outward towards some external world or paradise. If they realized the ultimate reality of life within themselves, then even this world would become an eternally peaceful land.

His life itself was a teaching, an example of the path to enlightenment & his death a teaching on impermanence. His teachings led people towards the understanding of the Mystic Law

## NICHIREN DAISHONIN

Nichiren Daishonin is known as the Original or true Buddha of the Latter Day. He gave concrete & practical expression to the Buddhist philosophy of life that was taught by Shakyamuni and illuminated by his disciples over the years. He was born on February 16, 1222 in Japan. He appeared in order to spread the teachings of Shakyamuni in a manner accessible by all people. He was born in the opening era of the "Latter Day of the Law" (mappo), a period of great suffering in those times. He took the name Nichiren which means Sun Lotus and was given the title of Daishonin (great sage) by his followers. As a young priest he had already become intuitively enlightened to the Law and spent the next two decades seeking documentary evidence to support his realization from the various sutras and documents that were available at that time. He became convinced that the true essence of Shakyamuni's teachings, the entity of the Law, was only contained in the Lotus Sutra, which is regarded as his highest teaching. He completely and thoroughly clarified the ultimate reality of life, the entity of the Law and defined this entity as Nam Myoho Renge Kyo. Nichiren's independent studies led him to conclude that the Lotus Sutra contained the only true way to salvation and that chanting the phrase "Nam Myoho Renge Kyo" is the way to attain enlightenment

His first pronouncement of Nam Myoho Renge Kyo was in 1253 and in 1279, finally realizing the purpose of his advent into this world, he inscribed the Dai Gohonzon. The Lotus Sutra predicts that during the latter day of the Law – a period of great turmoil – the Bodhisattvas of the Earth will appear to bring salvation to all mankind. The leader of these Bodhisattvas is Nichiren Daishonin who embodied the Mystic Law or ultimate reality of the universe, Nam Myoho Renge Kyo.

During the years of his teachings, Nichiren had to ensure that his followers grasped certain key cardinal points about Buddhism in order to fully understand and appreciate the significance of the Dai Gohonzon. They had to realize that a) The Lotus Sutra is paramount among all the teachings of Shakyamuni. b) To practice the Lotus Sutra is to chant Nam Myoho Renge Kyo c) Nichiren Daishonin was the true votary of the Lotus Sutra as contained within the predictions made in the Lotus Sutra d) The mission of all Buddhas is to save others from suffering, even in the face of extreme adversities.

Nichiren Daishonin drew a direct line between his Buddhism & that of Shakyamuni by basing the Gohonzon so closely to the 'Ceremony in the Air' and in doing so clarified the object of worship & the Law, which Shakyamuni alluded to during the ceremony.

Shakyamuni revealed his own experience of attaining enlightenment, the harvest of seeds sown in the past, without actually defining how he arrived at this state, nor the Law which he had realized. Nichiren Daishonin has stated that this Law is, and will always be, Nam Myoho Renge Kyo, and that anyone who chants this phrase to the Gohonzon can become enlightened in his lifetime. From this perspective, Shakyamuni can be said to have taught the Buddhism of 'harvest', or True Effect, while Nichiren Daishonin teaches the Buddhism of 'sowing' or True Cause.

# HISTORY

## 1. TEACHINGS OF SHAKYAMUNI

Shakyamuni expounded a great many teachings during his lifetime, concerning the wisdom of life & attitudes of faith, according to the various needs of his disciples. After his death his teachings were orally transmitted by his disciples for a great many years. Since precepts were required, to maintain discipline in monastic orders, it is likely that the Hinayana teachings were first recorded in sutra form. Shakyamuni's other teachings, free from precepts, were recorded later. It is not very clear when the teachings on the Ultimate Truth in the form of the Lotus Sutra was first compiled, but Nichiren Daishonin states in the Gosho that this was done fairly soon following Shakyamuni's death. Since Shakyamuni's teachings had already spread far and wide, this is probably why so many different forms of Buddhism exist today.

In the Lotus Sutra, Shakyamuni directed us to a source of power which can sever the chains of karmic forces. He left a guidepost to lead the people to his true intentions. In the Sutra of Infinite Meaning (Muryogi), it is stated that the Lotus Sutra reveals the ultimate truth of Shakyamuni's enlightenment and is supreme among all his teachings. All other Buddhist scriptures are partial and considered preparatory & it is the Lotus Sutra that gives meaning to all the others & explains the fundamental Law of Life.

## 2. SPREAD OF BUDDHISM

Buddhism spread throughout India following Shakyamuni's death, and then to neighboring countries. About 100 years after his death a rift arose amongst the Buddhist community resulting in two major streams of Buddhism. It spread in two main directions. The first through Sri Lanka, Burma, Thailand, Cambodia and other Southeast Asian countries and the second through Central Asia, via the Hind Kush, to China, Korea & Japan. The first stream is known as Southern Buddhism (Hinayana) while the second stream is known as Northern Buddhism (Mahayana). Southern Buddhism follows the tenets & rituals of early Buddhist teachings while undergoing minor changes influenced by various external cultures etc. The Northern stream underwent dramatic changes which were influenced by national and cultural characteristics, and evolved considerably in respect of its doctrines and rituals. Around 500 years after Shakyamuni's death, the spread of Buddhism was centered in Central Asia. During this period Buddhists established higher systems of Buddhist theory which they termed as the Mahayana Buddhism (Great vehicle) while criticizing the traditional early teachings & precept centered schools, labeling them Hinayana Buddhism (Lesser vehicle). It was approximately 500 years after the advent of Buddhism in China that the great teacher T'ien-T'ai established the doctrine of Ichinen Sanzen on the basis of the Lotus Sutra. Buddhism in Japan is said to have entered the Latter Day of the Law around 2000 years after the death of Shakyamuni. The various schools lauded the power of the Buddha as expounded in the sutras and denying the need to pursue doctrinal studies and the practice of Buddhism. The orthodox lineage of Buddhism was all but lost in this era. In India, Buddhism all but died out following the advent of Islam. In China, following the death of T'ien-T'ai and the Mongol invasion, Buddhism fell into a state of disorder. In the midst of all this confusion and decline of Northern Buddhism, Nichiren Daishonin appeared and established a new sect of Buddhism which would illuminate the darkness of the Latter Day of the Law.

### 3. MAHAYANA & HINAYANA BUDDHISM

Buddhism developed in India & divided into two main streams. The form of Buddhism first encountered by Westerners was called "Hinayana", the literal meaning of which is the 'lesser vehicle'. This form of Buddhism places great emphasis to strictly following the doctrine and practice and being monastic in that it stresses adherence to precepts & urging people to extinguish all desires. In one way it may even be termed as nihilistic, as it expounds the senselessness &

uselessness of life. Its application to daily life is limited, as to extinguish desires means to extinguish one's existence in this world. This has tended to reinforce the idea, already inherent in the Hinayana form, that Buddhism involves the shedding of material possessions and diligent monastic study adhering to strict physical & mental discipline to achieve a "higher reality" of life.

The other main stream of Buddhism is known a "Mahayana", the literal meaning of which is the 'greater vehicle'. This is so called because apart from being concerned with individual salvation, it also stresses the importance of leading ALL people towards enlightenment. It focuses on the need for this, to be a religion of the common people, who are capable of helping themselves to tackle the day to day realities of life and living.

The teachings of Mahayana Buddhism are subdivided into two parts. The first is termed as 'provisional' Mahayana Buddhism, which resembles some aspects of Christianity, teaching of 'pure and mystical lands' & to believe in a transcendental being and obtaining salvation through the offices of legendary Bodhisattvas & Buddhas. In some schools of thought this form of Buddhism has been termed as being similar to escapism, in that it generally seeks happiness & meaning in not this world, but in some mythical paradise or nirvana of transcendental beings.

Little is known of 'true" Mahayana Buddhism in the West. This form of Buddhism is the basis of Nichiren Daishonin's Buddhism which states that the supreme teachings of Shakyamuni is the Lotus Sutra and that enlightenment is inherent within each one of us. True Mahayana Buddhism leads to a reformation within the human being itself.

Simply put, early (provisional) Mahayana teachings asserted that it was impossible to obtain enlightenment in this impure world & set forth practice so that one can obtain rebirth in ideal worlds such as the 'Pure land of perfect bliss'. Later (true) Mahayana teachings state that it is possible to carry out Bodhisattva practices, such as the six paramitas, in this world even though it may take many many kalpas to attain enlightenment. The Lotus Sutra reveals that all people can obtain enlightenment in this lifetime. By embracing the Mystic Law, one can obtain the benefits of the six kinds of practices and thus obtain enlightenment early. Pre Lotus Sutra teachings identifies a universal self, visualized in the form of a personality, while the Lotus Sutra identifies this universal self or reality as extant within ourselves and regards this reality as the "Law", which Nichiren Daishonin interpreted as Nam Myoho Renge Kyo.

Hinayana teachings state that earthly desires and existence must be extinguished. This is even adhered to by followers of early provisional Mahayana teachings. In contrast the Lotus Sutra, as interpreted by Nichiren Daishonin, established a way for all people to challenge and overcome the sufferings of this world and show the way to freedom from selfishness & self-righteousness based upon the universal law.

## 4. NOTABLE BUDDHIST SCHOLARS

Nikko Shonin – (6th century BC). He accurately preserved and propagated the teachings of Shakyamuni Buddha.
Kumarajiva – (344 – 413 AD). He translated the Lotus Sutra from Sanskrit to Chinese. This translation is deemed by Nichiren Daishonin, to be the most accurate translation.
T'ien T'ai – (531 – 597 AD). He systemized the teachings of the Lotus Sutra.
Dengyo – (767 – 822 AD). He is the creator of the Tendai sect in Japan and is responsible for bringing T'ien T'ai Buddhism to Japan. He established the Lotus Sutra as the most supreme of Shakyamuni's teachings.

## 5. THREE STAGES OF PROPAGATION – FORMER/MIDDLE/LATTER DAYS

The spread of Buddhism, like any religion, can be divided into 3 stages, according to the degree in which people are influenced. The first period brings forth solutions & salvation from which to alleviate the people of their sufferings and problems. The second period is akin to when the religion is established within society and at times taken for granted and as matter of fact. The third stage is when the religion becomes ineffective and loses its power to enlighten and redeem humanity from despair, alienation & other problems. These three stages are known as the Former Day of the Law, The Middle Day of the

Law & the Latter Day of the Law. The first two stages are said to have lasted 1000 years each while the present is the Latter Day of the Law.

## 6. BUDDHISM IN INDIA

In accordance with Shakyamuni's predictions, the propagation of his teachings was expounded by twenty four successors who inherited his lineage over 1000 years after his death. Early Buddhism was centered round North Eastern India and based on Hinayana teachings before spreading throughout India and being intermixed with some elements of Mahayana teachings. The latter part of the Former Day of the law saw the exclusive spread of Mahayana teachings, and spreading as far as Northern Afghanistan. However in Southern India, Hinayana Buddhism maintained a steady influence, which laid the foundation for its spread throughout South East Asia right until the present times of the Latter Day of the Law.

## 7. BUDDHISM IN CHINA

Buddhism reached China from India via the Silk Road and around the time of the start of the Christian era. By then Confucianism and Taoism were already established in China. The teachings of Confucius stressed the need for order & harmony of human relationships. Taoism is based on the teachings of Lao Tzu and highly values life which is in harmony with nature

& noninterference with the course of natural events. Many Chinese priests went to India to seek Buddhist teachings & many Indian priests also went to China, dedicating themselves to the translation of the scriptures. Buddhism, after being transmitted to China, underwent changes within the Chinese spiritual environment and was systemized and formulated into a philosophical system. This also led to a variety of opinions being flaunted as to which sutras of Shakyamuni were most profound and contained his true intentions. It was the great scholar T'ien-T'ai who organized the innumerable sutras and established a system of classification. He also established the supremacy of the Lotus Sutra, which was earlier translated by Kumarajiva. T'ien-T'ai established the profound doctrine of Buddhism on the basis of Myoho Renge Kyo – the translation of the Lotus Sutra. Nichiren Daishonin considered this as the best among the translations of the Lotus Sutra & used this to expound his teachings. When Buddhism was introduced into China, all the sutras were translated into classical Chinese. The Chinese translation of the Lotus Sutra is "Miao-fa Lien-hua Ching."

## 8. BUDDHISM IN JAPAN

Buddhism made its advent in Japan via Korea around a thousand years after the death of Shakyamuni. In those days Japan had no religious system but followed the practice of ancestor & nature worship. Buddhism came to co-exist with the worship of Shinto Gods similar to the co-existence of Buddhism in China with Confucianism & Taoism. In due course of time Buddhism began to spread & became the spiritual basis of the nation with widespread belief in the Lotus Sutra. Many sutras were bought into Japan via China which also led to the establishment of various Hinayana sects together with sects based on Mahayana teachings. This led to Buddhism being changed from a state religion to a sect based religion. Buddhism in Japan underwent a constant change in the popularity of various Buddhist sects, such as the Shingon, Jodo & Zen sects, leading to religious & social ferment. It was in these troubled times that Nichiren Daishonin appeared to propagate his Buddhism which is based on the doctrines of T'ien-T'ai & Dengyo. Nichiren Buddhism goes beyond the framework of Chinese Buddhism which in turn had surpassed the limited ways of thinking of Indian Buddhism.

## 9. BUDDHIST SECTS IN JAPAN

A great many Buddhist sects have come and gone in Japan, with many existing today. During the Nara period (710-794), six schools of Buddhism flourished, which were the Kegon, Hosso, Kusha, Jojitsu, Ritsu & Sanron sects. Of these, the Kegon, Hosso & Ritsu sects are still in existence today. Later, the Tendai sect was founded by Dengyo, based on the Lotus Sutra, and around the same time the Shingon sect was founded by Kobo, based on the Dainichi (Mahavairochana) sutra. At some stage, the Tendai sect fell under the influence of the Shingon sect and underwent changes. The Tendai sect, mixed with various esoteric teachings, is called Tendai esotericism (Taimitsu), while the Shingon sect in direct line of Kobo is known as Eastern esotericism (Tomitsu). Around the end of the Heian (794-1185) period the Jodo (Nembutsu) sect was founded by Honen, based on the practice of reciting the name of Amida Buddha as the only means by which to attain rebirth in the Pure Land. The Zen sect was established during the Kamakura period (1185-1333).

The six sects of Nara together with the Shingon & Tendai sects are collectively referred to as the eight sects and these, with the Nembutsu & Zen sects, are frequently referred to in the Gosho, as the ten major sects of Buddhism in Japan.

## 10. <u>NICHIREN SOSHU (ORTHODOX NICHIREN SECT)</u>

Nichiren Daishon had designated Nikko Shonin as his successor, before his death. Nikko Shonin was the only disciple of Nichiren Daishonin who followed & propagated his teachings faithfully. Nichiren Daishonin wrote many treatises & letters to his followers, which were collected & kept safely by Nikko Shonin, thus preserving his teachings. These collection of his writings, are called the Gosho. The Buddhism propagated by Nichiren Daishonin lived on through various turbulent times and came to be known as Nichiren Shoshu (Orthodox Nichiren sect). The Dai-Gohonzon is enshrined in the temple at Taisekiji. Recently, with the advent of the Soka Gakkai & the freedom of religion in Japan, has led to, a remarkable development of Nichiren Buddhism in Japan & throughout the world.

## 11. <u>SOKA GAKKAI</u>

The Soka Gakkai was founded in 1930 by Tsunesaburo Makiguchi, who became its first president, & Josei Toda, his disciple. The organization was based on the faith in Buddhism as taught by Nichiren Daishonin & first was known as the Value Creating Education Society. In 1943 because of the opposition to the government's policy in regard to religion, President Makiguchi & General Director Toda, along with twenty one other disciples were arrested & incarcerated. President Makiguchi died in prison in 1944. After release from prison, Josei Toda set about rebuilding the organization under the new name "Soka Gakkai" whose aim was to solely propagate the Buddhism of Nichiren Daishonin throughout the world. The practical basis of Soka Gakkai is to spread & awaken in the people, Buddhism, as a 'life philosophy, providing links of faith spanning the world, to maintain the purity of Nichiren Daishonin's teachings, helping members to correctly practice & thus creating the maximum happiness and value for both themselves & others, focusing on "kosen rofu" – creating value in each area of society. The Soka Gakkai International (SGI) was created by Daisaku Ikeda in 1975 and later incorporated as an NGO of the United Nations. SGI is the name given to the lay organizations throughout the world which practice Nichiren Buddhism. As explained by Daisaku Ikeda – "The organization is necessary in order for many people to advance together in harmony.... All in all, solitary practice does not bring about correct faith, practice & study, or a correct relationship between the individual & society based on the Mystic Law..... If you realize the importance of people encouraging each other to maintain their faith and to live courageously, then you will naturally understand the importance of the organization as a means to practice correctly." SGI activities are based on the principle of itai doshin, which means, "many bodies, one mind". This specifically refers to the unity of purpose that many people can achieve, through kosen rofu, and ultimately their own human revolution.

# NICHIREN BUDDHISM

"THE PURPOSE OF OUR PRACTICE OF NICHIREN BUDDHISM & OUR FAITH IN THE MYSTIC LAW OF NAM MYOHO RENGE KYO ENABLES US TO ESTABLISH A STATE OF ETERNAL HAPPINESS IN OUR LIVES."

# A). GENERAL CONCEPTS

## 1. The Need for Religious Philosophy

Everyone wants to be fulfilled & happy. With the increased access to new technology & communications, we are learning more about the world around us. However the world which lies within us still remains a mystery. Many people claim to know themselves, but this often means that we know our failings & weaknesses. It is true, that in order to lead better lives, objective cognition is necessary. However it is the extent of how effectively we use this method, to improve our lives, that decides the degree to which we are awakened to the truth that lies in the depth of our lives. This truth is what Buddhism elucidates. Buddhism illuminates our lives with an awareness of our potential rather than our limitations, which enables us to tackle the difficulties in our lives and to go forth into society with hope & courage.

## 2. Faith, Benefit, Happiness

One of the underlying assumptions of Buddhism is that everyone can and must strive to be united with the Law, directly & not through an intermediary, by becoming a Buddha. It is only through faith that one can attain the Buddha wisdom, dormant & inherent in each of us. Belief means acceptance of a truth or premise but not blind obedience. Buddhism rejects the notion of faith in an individual being. The object of faith is the Universal law, immanent in both, our lives and the cosmos. The Chinese character for faith has two meanings – not to deceive & not to doubt. There is no such thing as 'blind faith' in Nichiren Buddhism. Great emphasis is placed on what one practices & why

As Nichiren Daishonin states – "To believe in the perfect teaching means to awaken faith through doctrine and make faith the basis of practice."

The purpose of Buddhism is to enable all people to attain the same state as the Buddha, to attain supreme wisdom, thus awakening them to the universal Law to which the Buddha is enlightened. This is what "Buddhahood" is, the ultimate benefit of faith. What are termed benefits are the results of life's inner changes. Nichiren Daishonin defines "benefit" as the purification of the six senses, saying in effect that benefit lies in the purification of all the mental & physical functions of life. Benefits are divided into two categories: Wisdom, which indicates the reformation of human life (shoho) and Good Fortune, which means the reformation of one's environment (eho), more commonly termed as inconspicuous & conspicuous benefits.

Happiness is directly related to the degree that one can draw on their own life force & the hope one has for the future. All human activities aim at happiness. Buddhism shows the way to develop the wisdom, challenging the difficulties that one faces and to surmount the same, thus developing one's life force. It is this attitude that leads to absolute & lasting happiness. The purpose of our Buddhist practice & faith in the Mystic Law is to establish a state of eternal happiness in our lives.

As a learned sage once said "What is happiness? Though there is happiness that comes from without, genuine happiness comes from within."

## 3. The law of Causation (Cause & Effect)

The law of causation is the universal principle underlying all visible and invisible phenomena and events in daily life

The concept of causation is known in Sanskrit as *pratiya-samut-pada* and in Japanese as *engi*, which literally means, "dependent origination'. This law explains that the fundamental process whereby all sentient beings & phenomena in the universe exist as a result of causes. All things in the universe are subject to this law of cause & effect and consequently nothing can exist independently of other things or arise of its own accord. Needless to say, this web of causation that binds all things is temporal as well as spatial, so that not only are all things in existence at the present moment, dependent on one another, but also dependent on all things existing in the past & future as well. Buddhism asserts that each individual is responsible for his own destiny &

at the same time has the prerogative to change it for the better and develop his character in the future. If we stand firmly on the riverbed of life, the Mystic Law, that is the entity of life, not even the torrents of destiny can carry us away.

Cause & effect is a principle which is probably taken for granted by each of us in our lives.

In the past before the advent of scientific rationality, most effects whose causes we could not comprehend were taken to be a form of God's work or magic. Today, with scientific rationale available most phenomena are explained as particular effects of particular causes. However even today, the inability to discern cause & effect in all phenomena has led to the deduction of the existence of God or a transcendental force, at least to provide the 'First Cause', which set everything & all life into motion.

Buddhism teaches that everything in the universe embodies the law of cause & effect. Nothing is the cause of a celestial being or mere chance. Buddhism denies the idea of 'First Cause', just as there will be no final end. This is the Buddhist conception of 'time without beginning or end'.

However certain aspects of life do seem to operate outside the pattern of cause & effect, such as the different conditions that one is born into, luck, tragedies and the various diversities of fate that exist between each of us. This leads to the perfectly good argument of the existence of chance. The Buddhist concept of causality goes much deeper than mere chance & this involves probing the depths of our lives for the inherent cause & the latent effects that we subjectively experience and which in turn leads to interaction with the environment that we inhabit.

Manifested effect always follows a cause, irrespective of the delay between the two. This leads to the theory that one always follows the other leading to an unbroken line of cause & effect relationships though time. At a more deep level, cause & effect are simultaneous, for just as we experience effects now resulting from causes made in the past, so too are we making causes which will show manifested effects in the future. As Nichiren Daishonin states – "There can be no discontinuity between past, present & future."

This leads to the distinction between two different, but closely connected types of cause & effect – External cause & Manifest effect AND Inherent cause & Latent effect. Simply put, external cause & manifest effect are perceived in the physical (seen) (Ke) (1st-7th consciousness) world while inherent cause & latent effect lie within the spiritual (unseen) (Ku) (8th consciousness) world. Buddhism explains that in common to all phenomena, cause & effect is subject to the rhythm of life & death just as life & death is subject to the law of cause & effect. The simultaneity of cause & effect teaches that the moment we take action as a result of a combination of external cause & our own inherent cause, the latent effect of that is lodged in our lives to appear as a manifested effect, when meeting the right external cause at some point in the future.

Recognizing the existence of an inherent cause leads to the development of a strong desire to change it so that we can make the right external cause to get the effects that we want to see. HOWEVER one must bear in mind that not all is condoned. Buddhist doctrine teaches that one who degrades life or creates suffering for others will have made the external cause for which one must inevitably experience the effect of suffering himself, in the future. As Nichiren Daishonin says – "One who climbs a mountain must eventually descend. One who slights another will, in turn be despised."

Inherent cause gives rise to latent effect which is also known as 'karma'.

In addition our inherent causes attract like minded effects. Such as hunger within attracts hunger without, while often repelling those who are not hungry.

Once the strictness of the Law of cause & effect is understood, it can be used to fundamentally change one's negative karma, so as to stop experiencing & creating suffering in their lives and others, by making the right causes to experience happiness now and in the future. Cause & Effect exist simultaneously. The nine worlds (stage of cause) and the world of Buddhahood (stage of effect), exist simultaneously in our lives.

Chanting, Nam Myoho Renge Kyo to the Gohonzon, is the cause which immediately has the effect of releasing the innate Buddhahood which lies inherent within us, thus purifying our inner spirit that motivates positive action.

## 4. Buddhahood

Enlightenment means to come to a complete awareness of the inherent Buddhahood within each of us. The awakening of this state in our lives brings with it such characteristics such as strengthened energy, courage, determination, compassion & wisdom. The Lotus Sutra teaches that belief in the teachings is a means to attain enlightenment, while Nichiren Daishonnin's Buddhism teaches that belief in itself is enlightenment. There are no commandments whatsoever in Nichiren Daishonin's Buddhism, since an awakening to our Buddhahood enables us to make our own oral & ethical judgments. The Lotus Sutra leads people towards the understanding of the Mystic Law, whereas Nichiren Daishonin embodied the Mystic Law, Nam Myoho Renge Kyo in the Gohonzon. The Lotus Sutra specified the principle of attaining Buddhahood in this lifetime & Nichiren Daishonin revealed & manifested the Law – Nam Myoho Renge Kyo – thus showing the way to attain Buddhahood.

Contrary to general belief & perceptions, enlightenment is not something removed from or alien to ordinary human existence. Life that pervades the universe, (Ichinen Sanzen – Three thousand realms of existence in a single moment of life), exists in each individual. Enlightenment is the merging of the states of Buddhahood existing in the universe & inherent in ourselves.

As Daisaku Ikeda clarifies, "What does attaining Buddhahood mean for us? It does not mean that we suddenly turn into a Buddha or become magically enlightened. In a sense attaining Buddhahood means that we have securely entered the path or orbit, of Buddhahood inherent in the cosmos. Rather than a static final destination at which we arrive and remain, achieving enlightenment means firmly establishing the path needed to keep advancing along the path of absolute happiness limitlessly, without end." Buddhahood exists and can only be manifested, here and now through the actions of real people in this real world.

## B). BUDDHIST DOCTRINE

1. <u>The Law</u>

Shakyamuni propagated that all people should rely on the Law as their teacher rather than a sentient being. The Sanskrit word being 'Dharma" symbolizing the Law, that which is the truth underlying all phenomena. The Law has not been laid down by any specified being, but has inherently existed as the core of the universe. Shakyamuni realized and taught the Law and Nichiren Daishonin clarified the same in its entirety – that is Nam Myoho Renge Kyo itself.

There exist many truths, extending from the specific or phenomenal to the universal & essential. At the deepest level of life, the fundamental truth which supports all universal phenomena & laws is the Mystic Law as indicated in the Lotus Sutra. .

The Buddha neither created nor laid down the Law, but clarified the Law originally governing the universe. The Law is like the truth within the realm of natural sciences rather than like the laws of jurisprudence. To view Buddhist Law in this way gives one an insight that penetrates the truth underlying the nature of all phenomena. In this sense the Universal Law is the reason of all existence.

The Law means the teachings expounded by Buddha. By practicing this Law, all people can attain Buddhahood. In Nichiren Buddhism the Law is the Gohonzon.

Buddhism teaches that everything in the universe is an expression of, and acts in accordance with the Law. It is important to learn of the existence of the Law, even if we do not understand it theoretically. Simply chanting Nam Myoho Renge Kyo, reveals the Law in our lives and puts us in rhythm & harmony with this universal law.

Have faith, belief & chant Nam Myoho Renge Kyo sincerely, and you will see the benefits of the Law in terms of actual proof. The Mystic Law, Nam Myoho Renge Kyo transcends time & place.

2. <u>Ichinen Sanzen</u>

Ichinen Sanzen indicates the entity of life and the varying aspects & phases it assumes. All physical & mental activities are functions that are expressed by life, & not life itself. This is the entity of life and which is beyond the comprehension of science or logic.

Ichinen Sanzen is an integration of all life's phenomena, into a single system, consisting of:

a) Ten Worlds
b) Mutual Possession of the Ten Worlds
c) Ten Factors of Life
d) Three Realms of Existence,

Ichinen Sanzen literally means "three thousand realms in a single moment of life".

Ichinen Sanzen explains theoretically how,

by changing yourself, you change the world around you. We are all part of many different and overlapping societies, each with our own individual karma and identity which is inextricably linked with that of other beings.

Difficult as it may seem, the highest levels of Buddhist philosophy teach that non sentient beings are also capable of attaining Buddhahood. When acted upon by sentient beings the Ten Worlds of the non sentient beings are revealed. When a sentient being attains Buddhahood, the same state of life is simultaneously manifested by its surroundings, bringing out Buddhahood from within insentient beings in accordance with the principle of life and its environment.

The Ten Worlds, their Mutual Possession, the Ten Factors & the Three Realms of Existence, when multiplied together create the 3,000 aspects of life or all life's phenomena. The entity of life, with its 3,000 changing conditions (aspects) of all phenomena at every moment, is the ultimate reality of life, the Mystic Law – NAM MYOHO RENGE KYO.

Nam Myoho Renge Kyo indicates the entity of life in terms of the three thousand changing conditions of phenomena. It can be stated that the three thousand constantly changing aspects of life in any given moment is Nam Myoho Renge Kyo.

As Nichikan Shonin (26th high priest of Nichiren Shoshu) explains – "Three thousand realms in a single moment of life, has two meanings according to the Lotus Sutra: 'to contain' & to 'permeate'. The entire universe is contained in each life at every moment of its existence. Conversely, each life moment permeates the entire universe. "The life moment is a particle of dust holding the elements of all worlds in the universe. It is a drop of water whose essence differs in no way from the vast ocean itself."

The doctrine of three thousand realms in a single moment is the path to Buddhahood. It is the condition of simultaneity of cause & effect that we realize in our lives through our concentrated prayer or mind of faith. It is a condition in which the Nine Worlds (Cause) and the World of Buddhahood (Effect) exist simultaneously in a single moment of life. Nichiren Daishonin likens such a state to a 'jewel' because it embodies the mutual possession of the Ten Worlds within the 3000 realms, and shines with beautiful gem like brilliance. The essence of such a state of life is none other than our steadfast and strong faith in the Mystic Law (Nam Myoho Renge Kyo). Our concentrated prayer is manifested as a jewel that contains Buddhahood.

3. <u>The Ten Worlds</u>

The Ten Worlds are potential life conditions, inherent in everyone, and which we experience moment to moment. Each has, both, positive & negative aspects, with the exception of Buddhahood, which is wholly positive.

    a.    Hell

-ve - This is condition of suffering, devoid of

freedom and with very little life force. One feels trapped by one's circumstances, dominated by frustrated rage and with an urge for destruction.

+ve - Hell enables one to identify with happiness, the suffering of others and striving to ensure that one does not fall into this life condition

### b. Hunger

-ve - This is a condition characterized by being under the sway of desires for materialistic possessions and excesses which do not abate even when one's desires are fulfilled.

+ve - Hunger is the driving force and ignites desire in one to get things done.

### c. Animality

-ve - This is a condition dominated by primal instinct, lack of morality & living for the moment.

+ve - Animality heightens our intuitive wisdom and our instincts to protect and nurture life, both our own and the lives of others around us.

### d. Anger

-ve - This is a condition dominated by arrogance, selfishness, unyielding competitiveness, conflicts & stubbornness.

+ve - Anger heightens our passionate energy, pursuit of excellence and abhorrence of injustice.

### e. Humanity (Tranquility)

-ve - This is a condition of laziness & characterizes lack of effort to rise to meet any challenge, a neutral state of peace & calm, a negative side of complacency.

+ve - Humanity enables one to make fair assessments, control instinctive desires and act in harmony with our surroundings.

### f. Rapture (Heaven)

-ve - This state is a temporary phase and is easily disrupted by any small change in circumstances. Even if things do not change the euphoria of rapture abates with the passage of time.

+ve - This is a condition of pleasure, as experienced when one's desires and wants are fulfilled.

MOST BEINGS SPEND THEIR TIME AND EXISTENCE MOVING BETWEEN THESE SIX LIFE CONDITIONS (WORLDS). THESE ARE ALSO KNOWN AS THE SIX LOWER WORLDS AND ARISE AUTOMATICALLY FROM WITHIN OUR LIVES IN RESPONSE TO EXTERNAL FACTORS IN OUR SURROUNDINGS.

### g. Learning

+ve -This is a condition in which one seeks skill, lasting truth and self improvement, through the teachings of others.

### h. Realization

-ve - Realization & Learning are similar and have the drawback that one can become supercilious and condescending.

+ve - This is a condition in which one discovers

a partial truth akin to the opening of one's eyes and through one's own initiative, observations, concentration and understanding

### i. Bodhisattva

-ve - Negatively it may cause one to neglect one's own life and to act merely out of a sense of duty.

+ve - This is a condition in which one aspires for personal enlightenment AND devotes oneself to alleviate the sufferings of others through compassionate and altruistic actions

### j. Buddhahood

This is the highest of the Ten Worlds and a condition of unparalleled pure and indestructible happiness, which is totally independent of one's circumstances. It is characterized by boundless compassion, wisdom, courage and life force.

THE FOUR HIGHER WORLDS ARE ALSO KNOWN AS "THE FOUR NOBLE PATHS".

Since each of the Ten Worlds possesses all the Ten Worlds within itself, each has the potential to reveal any of the others at any given moment. This enables us to reveal our Buddhahood from the very first moment we embrace the Mystic Law.

Originally, the Ten Worlds were viewed as separate locations each having its own set of inhabitants. The Lotus Sutra, however, teaches that each of the Ten Worlds is encompassed within each other thus interpreting them as potential states of life in each individual.

## 4. Mutual Possession of the Ten Worlds

The Mutual Possession of the Ten Worlds means that each of the ten states of life has the potential to express it as well as the other nine states. The Lotus Sutra rejects the notion that the Ten Worlds are separate from one another. Thus life is not fixed in any of the Ten Worlds but can manifest itself in any of the ten, at any given moment. The Mutual Possession of the Ten Worlds indicates the ever present possibility of transition from one condition to another.

Any one of the Ten Worlds can affect all the others. This is the theoretical basis for explaining the possibility of moving from one state to another, from moment to moment.

Each world contains the other nine worlds within itself, which brings us to the question of where the other worlds go to when we are in one world? Buddhism explains this by the concept of Ku, which shows that there are in a state of latency – neither existence nor non existence – which are activated at the right time and under the appropriate conditions.

The Mutual possession of the Ten Worlds is a component principle of three thousand realms in a single moment of life as set forth by T'ien T'ai in "Great Concentration & Insight."

## 5. The Ten Factors of Life

The Ten factors of Life are set forth in the Hoben chapter of the Lotus Sutra. While the Ten Worlds express the differences among phenomena, the Ten Factors describe the pattern of existence, common to all phenomena, which is manifested by the entity of life at each moment.

a. Appearance (Nyozeso) – The material aspects of our lives. This corresponds to the truth of temporary existence (Ke)
b. Nature (Nyozesho) – The inherent quality that cannot be seen or understood from the outside. This corresponds to the truth of non- substantiality (Ku)
c. Entity (Nyozetai) – The entity of life that permeates and manifests itself in its physical appearance & inner nature. This corresponds to the truth of the Middle Way (Chu)
d. Power (Nyozeriki) – Our inner strength, will and power to succeed.
e. Influence (Nyozesa) – Our acts & deeds when our latent energy is activated.
f. Internal Cause (Nyozein) – The latent cause in life which produces a corresponding effect of the same nature. Each internal cause contains a latent effect.
g. Relation (Nyozeen) – This is the function connecting life with its surroundings. When this external function is activated, internal causes are manifested into latent effects. Thus relation is viewed as the influence that enables one to make causes & experience their effects.
h. Latent Effect (Nyozeka) – This is the result

of the activation of internal cause by the function of 'Relation".

i. Manifest Effect (Nyozeho) – The perceived result that is manifested over a period of time as a consequence of Internal Cause & Latent Effect.

j. Consistency from beginning to End (Nyoze Hommatsu Kukyoto) – This is the integrating factor that unites the first nine factors, and comprises of a harmonious entity in every moment of life.

The first three factors are phases of life. Appearance & Nature are manifestations of entity. The next six factors are the functions of life. These are all interrelated as in a flow. Consistency integrates all the nine factors from beginning to end and thus termed as the entity of life.

A further commentary by Miao Lo on one of T'ien T'ai's major works states – "Appearance exists only in what is material, nature only in what is spiritual. Entity, power, influence and relation (external cause) in principle combine both the material & the spiritual. Inherent cause and latent effect are purely spiritual; manifest effect exists in only what is material." – The last of the Ten Factors is best explained by describing how the other nine factors work together and make up one harmonious whole.

## 6. The Three Realms of Existence

The Three Realms of existence analyzes life at three different levels & explains the distinctive characters of individual life forms.

The Three Realms of existence are:

a. The realm of the Five Components which analyze the functions of life which influences and assimilates its surroundings. The five components are Form (Shiki) – The body that perceives the outer world, Perception (Ju) – A comprehension & understanding of the information perceived, Conception (So) – Analyzing & forming an idea or definition on the data received, Volition (Gyo) – The will to initiate action based on one's conclusions, Consciousness (Shiki) – This is the entity which combines the other four components, and is the function of life which can make value judgments.

b. The realm of living beings. This is the temporary unification of the five components which form a living being, capable of experiencing the Ten Worlds. Since all living beings are in a state of interrelationship & reciprocal influence with one another, this realm can also be interpreted as the social environment of a living being.

c. The realm of environment. This is the basic environment that all livings beings exist in and which supports their existence.

Living beings contain the five components which work together in its consciousness (shoho), to interact with other living beings and the natural environment which together form (eho).
The Three Realms of Existence can be seen as the theoretical basis for (esho funi), which is the inseparability of the self and its environment.

## 7. The Three Truths

KU/KE/CHU (THE MIDDLE WAY)
The Three Truths are the truth of temporary, physical or material existence (ke), the truth of non-substantiality or the spiritual aspects of life (ku) and the truth of the Middle Way (chu) that is the force that binds and harmonizes ke & ku..
To put it differently, ke & ku are two different but inseparable aspects of chu.
The Buddhist concept decrees that all things are "phenomena". Uniting of constituent elements gives rise to phenomena and their separation brings about their dissolution. This is what is meant by the concept of non substantiality (Ku). The truth of non substantiality states that nothing exists independently but come into existence through their relationship with other things, known in Buddhism as 'dependent origination'. These united constituents appear as transient phenomena, in a constant flux, & known as a state of temporary existence (Ke).

As Shakyamuni stated "Decay is inherent in all composite things". Thus the internal nature of a single phenomena is Ku and its visible aspect can be thought of as Ke. All phenomena have the two aspects of Ku & Ke, and grasping phenomena with these two truths makes everything seem transitory, with no fixed existence of its own. This leaves too much to chance and is a contradiction of the perception of reality. Each of us has our own unique characteristics & qualities and this selective differentiation is the concept of the Middle Way (Chu). The concept of chu as based on the Lotus Sutra is known as the 'unification of the Three Truths". Ke & ku are expressions of the same entity which is alternating between its latent or manifested state. Which state this entity is at any given time is governed by the Mystic Law – chu or Nam Myoho Renge Kyo. To live a life of perfect balance, in which the physical & spiritual aspects of one's life function creatively, one has to follow the Middle Way – chu – which harmonizes and integrates both ke & ku.

Together Ku, Ke & Chu are known as the Three Truths and are a means to understand accurately, all phenomena in the universe. Enlightened wisdom (hoshin) relates to Ku, compassionate actions to relieve the sufferings of people (ojin) relates to Ke, and the essence of the Buddha's life (hosshin), or Nam Myoho Renge Kyo, relates to Chu. There exists an invisible & delicate thread of life which connects us with everything and everything with everything else. It consists of the Three Truths which in turn is one truth.

In early Buddhist teachings, the Middle Way

represented the path that transcends the two extremes of materialism (Ke) & spirituality (Ku). Rather than representing a compromise between opposites, it represents a path of perfect balance & value. In Nichiren Daishonin's Buddhism, the Middle Way is defined as Nam Myoho Renge Kyo, which is the essence of both the spiritual & physical aspects of life. KU / KE / CHU (The Middle Way)

8. <u>Karma</u>

Karma means "action" in Sanskrit – the language of the sutras. In Chinese this word was translated as the character 'ye' which means deeds, in the sense of achievements or results. Buddhism explains the concept of the continuing eternity of life. Life has existed forever in the cosmos, a continuous cycle. Sometimes manifest (lifetimes) and sometimes latent (death), known as the eternity if life. Karma is the accumulation of the good & bad causes that we bring with us from our former lives as well as the good & bad causes we have made in this lifetime, which shapes our future. This means that every mental, verbal & physical action imprints a latent effect on one's life. This 'karma' becomes manifest when activated by an external stimulus, and produces a corresponding effect. Our actions in the past have shaped our present and our actions in the present will shape our future. The law of karma exists over the three existences of the past, present & future. Buddhism does not consider one's karma or destiny to be fixed. Each individual has the potential to change the negative and positive aspects of their karma. Buddhism teaches that we have amassed negative & positive karma through countless lifetimes and we are experiencing the effects of this karma now and are continuing to recreate and reshape it. Nichiren Daishonin teaches that there is an area of our lives unaffected by karma – our Buddha nature and the practice of chanting Nam Myoho Renge Kyo is to reveal this area to ourselves.

We don't focus on our karma merely so that we may repay our karmic debt and bring our balance to zero. Rather, it is to convert our negative balance into a large positive balance. This is the principle of changing karma in Nichiren Buddhism.

The greatness of Nichiren Buddhism lies in the fact that by chanting Nam Myoho Renge Kyo, the shackles of one's karma are progressively weakened until they are severed completely.

Karma may be described as the fundamental tendency of our individual lives. Buddhism teaches that it is this karmic tendency of one's life which determines the nature & social world which they inhabit. This implies that any attempts to improve our circumstances are bound to end in failure if we do not simultaneously attempt to change the inherent tendencies within us which in turn have given rise to the circumstances which we are trying to improve. It is akin to one who is too lazy to wash and who tries to change his clothes in order to get rid of the unwashed smell.

There are only three possible reasons why people experience undeserved suffering & pain. It is, either, the will of God or a transcendental being, pure chance or the result of karma – the effects that they themselves have created. If it is the will of God, one can only reproach God for his lack of mercy. If it is chance then one can only feel resentful for fate having dealt such a blow. Admittedly one may alleviate their suffering but it is more common for one to sink into a sea of despair or apathy or in some cases, vent one's anger at someone or something. It is only logical to believe in this randomness if one denies the existence of the eternity of life and the continuity of cause and effect through the past, present & future.

Seen from the point of karma, it is extremely positive in that one is able to alter one's consequences for better or worse by further action. Karma is as much about the future as the past, if not more. Nichiren Buddhism teaches that we are continually creating future reality, which we then inhabit. So no matter what our suffering, by chanting Nam Myoho Renge Kyo, we can elevate our life condition and start to make good causes which will lead to our future happiness. If we encounter the right external causes and make the right choices, even deep seated karma can be changed. However it is inevitable that at some stage we must experience the bad effects of bad causes we have made in the past, either in this or previous lifetimes, but our actions now can noticeably reduce the impact of those effects. As Daisaku Ikeda explains – "A man's present state is not entirely determined by the immense, indefinite plexus of karmic causes inherited from the past. Although each human being inherits a karmic background from other existences, each is completely free to act in this world to alter it for better or worse, as he sees fit. Thus from a Buddhist view, man is innately free." This implies the important teaching that our decisions are not determined by our karmic tendencies, however much they may be influenced by them.

'As you give, so you receive', 'You reap what you sow', The 'Principle of Cause & Effect', are all examples of karma. Karma is a force that influences our present & future. Karma is manifested when activated by external stimuli (cause) & creates a corresponding action (effect).

Each individual is responsible for his own destiny & at the same time has the prerogative to change it for the better. One can effect changes in one's character, lifestyle, environment, philosophy, attitude, wisdom & life force. Our karmic actions in the past have determined our present and our current actions will determine our future. It is a fatalistic view that all things are predetermined. You are in charge of your own destiny. Live good qualities & you will receive, at sometime, an equivalent back into your life.

It is this comprehension and understanding which leads us to the path of positive action in creating positive causes which will ultimately lead to positive effects. In a word – KARMA.

## 9. Eternity of Life

The laws of cause & effect work within the eternal flow of life. The Lotus Sutra elucidated that it is possible to change one's destiny as well as the future by bringing forth this life from within us.

It is true that the eternity of life cannot be verified scientifically. However there are no scientific methods with which to grasp the essential quality of life itself, thus making it difficult to analyze the state in which life continues after physical death.

The Buddhist concept of eternal life, that is undergoing continuous change, is the most valid explanation for the disparities in the various fates of human beings. Although one accumulates many experiences, the essential reality of life neither, disappears or changes. Life carries on eternally and is dependent on the law of karma which operates over the past, present & future.

The Buddhist concept of the eternity of life places the life of an individual in the context of the universe as a whole. Since the universe exists in one form or the other throughout eternity, so too must all life contained within it exist eternally in one form or the other. Our lives have existed and will always exist simultaneously with the universe. Life & death are the alternating aspects in which our real self manifests itself, and both are part of the cosmic essence.

Nichiren Daishonin says - 'Myo' represents death & 'Ho' represents life. Life & death are two phases passed through by the entities of the Ten Worlds, the entities of all living beings which embody the law of cause & effect (renge). No phenomena are free from birth & death. Thus the life & death of all phenomena are simply the two phases of Myoho Renge Kyo.

The concept of Ku, Ke & Chu states that our lives are undergoing constant change, yet the inner core or our true self / entity remains constant. Based on this concept it is easy to understand the relationship between past identity, present identity & future identity, as starting before birth & continuing after death.

## 10. Nine Levels of Consciousness

Buddhism identifies nine levels of consciousness. The first five correspond to the five senses of sight, hearing, smell, taste & touch. The sixth makes a judgment about the physical & material world, the seventh (Mano) makes a judgment about the abstract (spiritual & mental) world, the eight (Alya) level stores our karma, the effects of all the causes we have made in this and our previous lifetimes. The ninth (Amala) level is the purity of our life force, our wisdom and compassion, the rhythm of the Mystic Law itself.

The first five consciousnesses enables us to receive information from the physical world, the sixth enables us to make a judgment based on the integration of the data received from/by the five senses, the seventh enables us to make abstract judgments based on the first six consciousness. The eight relates to our 'RAM' memory. This is where all our thoughts, deeds & words are recorded, from our present to our infinite past, whether we are consciously aware of it or not. This level of consciousness is not bound by time & space & remains limitless. This lies below the level of our conscious or waking mind but is constantly recording the experiences registered by the first seven consciousness levels & releasing information to us in the form of memories, hunches, likes, dislikes, feelings etc. The ninth consciousness is termed as 'the pure consciousness'. It is the very core of our lives – the inexhaustible life force of the universe. By chanting Nam Myoho Renge Kyo, the pure life force of the ninth consciousness permeates our entire being and purifies the other eight consciousnesses and also cleanses our negative karma. This is what sustains us throughout eternity.

## 11. <u>The Reality of Life</u>

The physical property of life corresponds to the temporary existence of the three truths. Life's essential nature cannot be grasped in the context of either non-substantiality or temporary existence. According to the Buddhist view, the universe is in itself in eternal existence, without beginning or end, a continuous uninterrupted flow as seen in the formation & collapse of stars and in the birth & death of living things. Yet throughout this eternal cycle, the essential reality of life never changes.

12. <u>General</u>

### a. Reality & Wisdom

'Kyo" is the 'reality' of the Buddha nature inherent in our lives. 'Chi' is the 'wisdom' to realize this truth. In the Latter Day the concept of 'kyo' is represented by the Gohonzon & 'chi' is represented by faith in the Gohonzon. Thus our Buddha nature is reality & our unflagging faith is wisdom. Accordingly the fusion of reality & wisdom is itself the attainment of Buddhahood.

### b. Three Powerful Enemies

They are commonly known as:

i) Ignorant people who denounce the Lotus Sutra.

ii) Learned people who falsely claim enlightenment

iii) Respected priests who act solely in their own selfish interests.

The "Encouraging Devotion" (13th) chapter of the Lotus Sutra describes three types of enemies who will persecute those who spread the sutra in the evil age which ensues after Shakyamuni's passing. They are defined by Miao-Lo in his treatise "The Words & Phrases of the Lotus

Sutra" & as stated in the concluding verses of the 'Encouraging Devotion" (13th) chapter as:
1. The arrogance & presumption of lay people – Those who are ignorant of Buddhism and who speak ill of those who propagate the sutras.
2. The arrogance & presumption of members of the Buddhist clergy – Insincere priests who though failing to understand the true essence of Buddhism, flaunt that they have attained the truth and scorn the practitioners of the sutra.
3. The arrogance and presumption of those who pretend to be sages – Revered priests who pretend to be sages but when fearful of losing their influence, fame and money entice authorities to persecute the practitioners of the Lotus Sutra.

### c. The Three Virtues

In the Gosho, (The Opening of the Eyes), Nichiren Daishonin states that these virtues of sovereign, teacher & parent are three categories that all people should respect and that which all Buddhas possess.

The virtue of sovereign means the power to protect and ensure the welfare of people and corresponds to the property of the Law (hosshin) which is inherent within life itself. The virtue of teacher is the power to give the people wisdom & knowledge, to make correct judgments and corresponds to the property of wisdom (hoshin)

The virtue of parent is the power to love, cherish, nurture & protect the people, enabling them to act & lead a fulfilling life. This corresponds to the property of compassion & action (ojin).

These three virtues represent the essential qualities for achieving true dignity as a human being. The Buddha is one who is eternally endowed with these virtues and manifests them completely.

### d. The Three Treasures

These are, the Buddha – one who has attained enlightenment, the Law – as expounded by the Shakyamuni, the Priesthood – those who preserve & propagate the Law. The treasure of the Buddha is Shakyamuni (Nichiren Daishonin). The treasure of the Law is the Lotus Sutra (Dai-Gohonzon). The treasure of the Priesthood is the various bodhisattvas & disciples propagating the Law.

### e. The Three Proofs

These are standards for judging the validity of doctrines and are known as documentary proof, theoretical proof & actual proof.

Documentary proof is actual evidence of the teachings and whether the ideas and teachings of Buddha are in agreement with the sutras. Thus any interpretation which is not based on the sutras cannot be considered Buddhist. Written evidence states that all Buddhist teachings lead to the Lotus Sutra and from there to Nam Myoho Renge Kyo and the Gohonzon.

Theoretical proof is whether the teachings are

within reason and logic and conforms to verifiable scientific findings and which refers to the actual evidence of the teachings. Learning about these profound teachings & principles, one comes to understand that Nam Myoho Renge Kyo perfectly elucidates the mysteries of life & death.

Actual proof is a measure whether the teachings expounded are borne by actual results & benefits when practiced. To see the positive effects & change that undergoes within a person's life. Profound belief in the doctrine comes only as a result of seeing actual proof or benefit, the effects of the practice

When any doctrine can measure up to these "proofs", it may be termed as valid and proven. Nichiren Daishonin states that he "has found that documentary & theoretical proofs are vital in judging the validity of Buddhist teachings, but that actual proof surpasses both."

## C). **LOTUS SUTRA**

1. Brief Overview

The Lotus Sutra is the primary teaching of Shakyamuni. It is a Mahayana sutra that reveals the true aspect of all phenomena, and maintains that all people can attain Buddhahood. The Lotus Sutra reveals the ultimate truth of Shakyamuni's enlightenment. It declares that all of Shakyamuni's previous teachings were preparatory. The Lotus Sutra has been expounded over the years by scholars such as Nagarjuna in India, T'ien-T'ai in China & Dengyo in Japan. The most widely honored translation of the Sanskrit texts is that by Kumarajiva. The Japanese title of Kumarajiva's translation is Myoho-Renge-Kyo (Lotus Sutra of the Wonderful Law). Amidst the turmoil of the early part of the Latter Day of the Law, Nichiren Daishonin appeared. Based upon his conviction of the supremacy of the Lotus Sutra amongst all of Shakyamuni's teachings, he stated that the essence of life is crystallized in the title of the Lotus Sutra. Chanting Nam-Myoho-Renge-Kyo is the correct Buddhist practice for the Latter Day of the Law, & by embodying his enlightened state in the Gohonzon, he also provided the way for the development of one's inherent Buddhahood. The Muryogi Sutra (Sutra of Infinite Meaning) & the Fugen Sutra (Sutra of Bodhisattva Fugen) are respectively the prologue & epilogue to the

Lotus Sutra. The former reveals that all principles & meanings come from the one Law and this will be revealed in the Lotus Sutra. The latter states that wisdom & enlightenment begins to function when a person is awakened to the one law as stated in the Lotus Sutra. The Lotus Sutra teaches that although all phenomena in the universe are impermanent, the ultimate reality permeating everything is eternally constant. These two sutras, together with the Lotus Sutra, have been designated by the great teacher Tien T'ai of China as the "Threefold Lotus Sutra".

The Lotus Sutra identifies a universal self that exists within us, within this world & throughout the universe. In Christianity & pre Lotus Sutra teachings, this universal self or ultimate reality is visualized in terms of a personality. The Lotus Sutra however regards this reality as the "Law" which governs everything. Shakyamuni cited the Law in the Lotus Sutra & Nichiren Daishonin identified this Law as Nam Myoho Renge Kyo.

The Lotus Sutra is the most profound of all Shakyamuni's teachings & gives meaning to all of his earlier sutras which only partially explain the fundamental Law of Life. The Lotus Sutra's preeminence amongst all of Shakyamuni's other sutras is contained in its philosophy that provides the theoretical explanation that all people can become Buddhas. The Lotus Sutra integrates Shakyamuni's doctrines into a far reaching philosophy which is called the Philosophy of Life.

The Sanskrit title of the Lotus Sutra is "Saddharna Pundarika Sutra". Saddharna means correct law,

Pundarika means white lotus & Sutra means the Buddha's teaching. The Chinese characters of the translation read as Miao-Fa-Lien-Hua-Ching & in Japanese the title reads as Myoho Renge Kyo.

The Lotus Sutra consists of 28 chapters, each chapter having its own specific name by which they are generally referred to. The first 14 chapters are known as the 'theoretical' teachings (Shakumon) of which the "Expedient Means" (2nd) chapter is its core. This chapter shows the potential of Buddhahood in every person's life. The next 14 chapters are known as the 'essential' teachings (Honmon) of which the "Life Span" (16th) chapter is its core. This chapter shows Buddhahood as manifested in the life of Shakyamuni. The theoretical teachings imply that the doctrines & principles remain in the realm of theory as long as they are viewed from the standpoint of the Buddha's transient identity. The essential teachings refer to the teachings expounded by the original Buddha who attained enlightenment in the remote past and as described in the Life Span chapter of the Lotus Sutra.

## Outline

The teachings of the Lotus Sutra are set and occur in what is known as the "Two places & Three Assemblies". The first assembly is convened atop Eagle Peak & starts with the "Introduction" (1st) chapter & continues through the first half of the "Treasure Tower" (11th) chapter. The second assembly is known as the "Ceremony in the Air" & starts with the latter half of the "Treasure Tower" (11th) chapter & ends with the "Entrustment" (22nd) chapter. The final assembly occurs back again atop Eagle Peak & starts with the "Medicine King" (23rd) chapter & continues through the "Universal Worthy" (28th) chapter, which is the conclusion of the Lotus Sutra.

The "Introduction" (1st) chapter describes the gathering of numerous persons including Bodhisattvas, Dragon kings, heavenly beings, Asuras etc. who have gathered at Eagle Peak to hear Shakyamuni Buddha preach. Shakyamuni enters into a state of 'samadhi' (A kind of meditation) at which stage various omens follow. He emerges from his meditation to begin his sermon. In the "Expedient Means" (2nd) chapter, Shakyamuni reveals that the purpose of Buddhas appearing in this world is to expound their teachings for the fundamental purpose of enabling all living beings to attain Buddhahood.

Shakyamuni further goes on to foretell that those who are gathered at Eagle Peak to hear the sutra and garner unshakable faith in its teachings shall attain Buddhahood in the future. This teaching declares that not only Bodhisattvas but also persons of learning (voice bearers) & realization (cause awakened ones) can attain Buddhahood, which was denied to them in the earlier sutras. This forms the basis of the theoretical teachings contained within the Lotus Sutra.

As events unfold, the question now is who will propagate the Lotus Sutra in the time after Shakyamuni's death. In the "Emergence of the

Treasure Tower" (11th) chapter, a huge ornate tower emerges from within the bowels of the Earth & rises into the air. Within the tower resides the "Buddha of Many Treasures". At the same time numerous bodhisattvas & Buddhas appear from the far corners of the universe and gather around the tower. Shakyamuni seats himself next to Buddha Many Treasures. The assembly atop Eagle Peak is now raised into mid air, where the Treasure Tower is suspended. Shakyamuni resumes his sermon, regarding who will have the responsibility of propagating the Lotus Sutra after his passing & teaching the principle of the six difficult & nine easy acts. These are a series of comparisons as set forth in the 11th chapter of the Lotus Sutra, which shows how difficult it is to embrace & spread the Lotus Sutra during the evil age which he predicts will ensue after his death.

The sutra goes on to show examples of evil people & women who have attained enlightenment, even though this possibility was denied in earlier sutras, & hence serve as an example to the gathered assembly to encourage the propagation of the sutra after Shakyamuni's passing. The Bodhisattvas & voice bearers, who are present, pledge & vow to propagate the sutra, overcoming the 'Three Powerful Enemies'. However, as recorded in the "Emerging from the Earth" (15th) chapter, Shakyamuni calls forth from within the Earth, innumerable Bodhisattvas whom he has been teaching since countless kalpas ago & to whom he entrusts the task of spreading the Lotus Sutra in the age after his passing.

These are the Boddhisattvas of the Earth. The appearance of these Boddhisattvas causes confusion & perplexity in the minds of those who are gathered. How could Shakyamuni have taught & converted this myriad of Boddhisattvas in the short span of his life??

In the "Life Span of the Thus Come One" (16th) chapter, Shakyamuni clarifies the true nature of his existence. He reveals that he attained enlightenment countless kalpas ago, since 'time without beginning'. He has been teaching & converting living beings in the real world during his many appearances in the real (saha) world as a Buddha. He teaches that to accept & believe in the Buddha who attained enlightenment in the distant past is a source of great benefit & virtue.

The sermon includes the story of Bodhisattva Never Disparaging, who was Shakyamuni Buddha in a past existence & to whom all Bodhisattvas should look to as a role model for respecting the ability & guiding all people to enlightenment.

In the "Supernatural Powers of the Thus Come One" (21st) chapter, Shakyamuni entrusts the Boddhisattvas of the Earth the specific task of propagating his teachings after his death. In the "Entrustment" (22nd) chapter, he urges all Bodhisattvas to propagate the Lotus Sutra. It suggests that what was expressed during this ceremony is the eternal & universal truth which transcends time & place. This concludes The Ceremony in the Air.

The assembly returns to Eagle Peak. The

gathering, including great Boddhisattvas such as 'Medicine King' & 'Universal Worthy' & other benevolent deities avow to safeguard the widespread propagation of the Lotus Sutra after Shakyamuni's death. As described in the "Universal Worthy" (28th) chapter, Shakyamuni concludes the preaching by instructing all present to accord the same greeting & respect to an upholder of the Lotus Sutra as he would to a Buddha.

The benefit of the Lotus Sutra is immense. The hand which takes it up immediately attains enlightenment and a mouth which chants it instantly enters Buddhahood, just as the moon is reflected on the water the moment it appears from behind the eastern mountains, or as a sound and its echo arise simultaneously. It is for this reason that the sutra states "Among those who hear of this Law, there is not one who shall not attain Buddhahood."

IN A NUTSHELL
The Lotus Sutra comprises of 28 chapters
Chapters 01 ~ 14 – Theoretical teachings
Chapters 15 ~ 28 – Essential teachings

Core of theoretical teachings – Chapter 2 (Expedient means)
Core of essential teachings – Chapter 16 (Life span of thus come one)
Theoretical teachings: The teachings of the Buddha (Shakyamuni) who attained enlightenment in his present lifetime.
Essential teachings : The teachings of the

true Buddha (Shakyamuni) who attained enlightenment, many kalpas ago.

Shakyamuni expounds his teachings in various settings, referred to as 'Two Places & Three Assemblies'. The 1st assembly is on Eagle Peak. The 2nd assembly is known as the 'Ceremony in the Air'. The 3rd assembly is back on Eagle Peak.

## 2. Hoben & Juryo Chapters

The Hoben (2nd) & Juryo (16th) chapters of the Lotus Sutra are regarded as the most important of all. In the Hoben chapter Shakyamuni expounds that all people have the potential to attain Buddhahood. In the Juryo chapter, he reveals that he attained enlightenment in the distant past & the implicit revelation of his attaining enlightenment.

This fundamental concept that enables all people to attain enlightenment is to be awakened to the eternally inherent ultimate law, Nam Myoho Renge Kyo, as taught by Nichiren Daishonin & revered by Shakyamuni.

The Hoben chapter is generally regarded as the means to manifest their Buddhahood & declares the preparatory nature of all of Shakyamuni's earlier teachings. This signifies that all earlier sutras contain partial truths and that the Lotus Sutra contains the entire truth. It also reveals that the life activities of all beings are the means by which they manifest Buddhahood. The Juryo chapter focuses on the depth &

duration of Shakyamuni's enlightenment. This also led to questions being asked as to why was Shakyamuni not born a Buddha, since he attained enlightenment in the distant past. The reason is that even when one has attained Buddhahood the other nine worlds are still present in his life. A Buddha is born into this world possessing the nine worlds and strives to attain the ultimate – Buddhahood. In this context, the Hoben chapter reveals that the nine worlds inherently possess Buddhahood, while the Juryo chapter reveals that Buddhahood retains the other nine worlds. They are necessary & integral components of life.

The recitation of the Hoben & Juryo chapters during gongyo expresses that the belief and faith that the inherent power of Nam Myoho Renge Kyo will become manifest & lead us towards Buddhahood. It also signifies our respect for Nichiren Daishonin who revealed the Law & made it possible for us to attain Buddhahood.

These two chapters are the apex of all the teachings expounded by Shakyamuni. The true aspects of the universe and all the principles of life are expounded in them, including the Three Truths (Ku/Ke/Chu); The Buddha's Three properties of the Law, wisdom & action; Eternal life which permeates the three existences of the past, present & future; The Ten Worlds; and the principle that earthly desires are enlightenment.

Hoben Chapter
Shakyamuni expounded his teachings, telling his disciples that, the wisdom of the Buddhas is immeasurable & difficult to understand. Why? A Buddha has attended to countless numbers of Buddhas & preaches the Law vigorously. The Law is profound & unknown. His intention is difficult to understand by some of his followers. Since Shakyamuni attained enlightenment, he has spread, through his various causes, his teachings & used many ways to guide living beings to be free from various desires & attachments and not to be fearful. Why & how? Because the Buddha has the perfection of wisdom, which is expansive & profound, Shakyamuni has awakened to the Law which has never been attained before. His teachings are skilful, soft, gentle, and delights the assembly. Shakyamuni has realized that this Law is limitless & boundless. He stops here. What he has attained is the rarest & most difficult to understand Law. This true entity of all phenomena (The Mystic Law), can be understood and shared between the Buddhas, and that all people have the potential to be Buddhas.

Juryo Chapter
At that time, when Shakyamuni decided to expound the fundamental Law, at his disciples' request, he told them to listen carefully to the teachings that lead people to enlightenment. The belief is that Shakyamuni attained enlightenment in Gaya, under the Bodhi tree, but in fact he attained enlightenment many countless kalpas ago, unlike as mentioned in the earlier sutras.

He explains the enormity of immeasurable time since he attained enlightenment. The Buddha dwells in the Land of Eternally Tranquil Light. The Buddha has through his emanations, guided untold number of living beings to happiness and enlightenment.

Shakyamuni speaks of the different methods and manifestations used to preach the Law, which are based on the receptiveness of 'living beings' and explains how, as an 'expedient means', he entered Nirvana. The Buddhas enter this world as various entities, to guide people and awaken them to the Buddha wisdom that exists in everyone. For those who have accumulated few causes for attaining Buddhahood, he uses 'expedient means' teachings, that he was enlightened in this lifetime, rather than eons ago, to cause them to enter the Buddha way. The Buddha's teachings are all true. He explains, to the beings of the 'Threefold Worlds', the entity of life without beginning or end. (The 'Threefold Worlds' are the Dharma world, the Bliss world, & the Manifested world). Because of the different natures, desires, actions & mentality of living beings, Shakyamuni employs different means to preach and guide them to enlightenment. This is the Buddha's work – unceasing. An immeasurable period of time has elapsed since the Buddha attained enlightenment & he will, throughout his immeasurable, eternal life span (Gohyaki-Jintengo), carry on taking action to lead people to Buddhahood.

Each day, events are activated as causes of 'Kuon Ganjo' (time without beginning), and we strive to achieve (effect) 'Ichinen Sanzen' (enlightenment – 3,000 realms of existence in a single moment of life). This is known as TRUE CAUSE & TRUE EFFECT.

To convey his meaning once more, Shakyamuni addressed his disciples in verse form (Jigage) Jigage portion of the Juryo (Life Span) chapter. The Jigage represents the soul of the 28 chapters of the Lotus Sutra.

Since attaining enlightenment many countless kalpas ago, the Buddha has constantly preached the Law, causing countless beings to enter the Buddha way. Shakyamuni uses 'expedient means' & his transcendental powers to guide the people to enlightenment over the three existences of past, present & future.

He uses entering Nirvana, as an 'expedient means' to make people wake up to their true self, renewing their faith & work towards enlightenment. This is the Buddha's power, to make people see the real beauty of the world we are in, irrespective of circumstances. The 'Real (Saha) World' & the 'Buddha World' are one and the same, perceived by different people, differently, depending on their beliefs. True belief opens the door to Buddhahood. This is the truth. Shakyamuni narrates the parable of the skilled physician & his sick children. When we sincerely believe in the Mystic Law, the Buddha manifests itself in us.

The Buddha's compassionate vow to lead us to enlightenment makes him appear to us in this world. His use of 'expedient means', as a tool of teaching, causes him to enter Nirvana, thus incorporating the two phenomena of life & death within the mystic workings of a single mind.

## 3. The Three Expedients

Shakyamuni gave many provisional teachings to his disciples as a means to lead them to his true teaching – the Lotus Sutra. These means or expedients that he used are broadly categorized into three groups. The first group consists of teachings he expounded depending upon the limitations of understanding & propensity of his disciples. The second group taught his disciples to be aware and sensitive to the sufferings of others and not to selfishly seek salvation for themselves only. In the third group he uses the Lotus Sutra to transmit the truth that he had realized.

# D) **CHAPTERS OF THE LOTUS SUTRA**

Chapters 1-14 Theoretical teachings (Shakumon)
Chapters 15-28 Essential teachings (Hommon)
Chapter 2 – Core of theoretical teachings
Chapter 16 – Core of essential teachings

| CHAPTER | JAPANESE | ENGLISH |
|---|---|---|
| 1 | JO | INTRODUCTION |
| 2 | HOBEN | EXPEDIENT MEANS |
| 3 | HIYU | SIMILE AND PARABLE |
| 4 | SHINGE | BELIEF AND UNDERSTANDING |
| 5 | YAKUSOYU | THE PARABLE OF THE MEDICINAL HERBS |
| 6 | JUKI | BESTOWAL OF PROPHECY |
| 7 | KEJOYU | THE PARABLE OF THE PHANTOM CITY |
| 8 | GOHYAKU DESHI JUKI | PROPHECY OF ENLIGHTENMENT FOR FIVE HUNDRED DISCIPLES |
| 9 | JU GAKU MUGAKU NINKI | PROPHECIES CONFERRED ON LEARNERS AND ADEPTS |

| | | |
|---|---|---|
| 10 | HOSSHI | TEACHER OF THE LAW |
| 11 | KEN HOTO | EMERGENCE OF THE TREASURE TOWER |
| 12 | DAIBADATTA | DEVADATTA |
| 13 | KANJI | ENCOURAGING DEVOTION |
| 14 | ANRA KUGYO | PEACEFUL PRACTICES |
| 15 | JUJI YUJUTSU | EMERGING FROM THE EARTH |
| 16 | NYORAI JURYO | LIFE SPAN OF THE THUS COME ONE |
| 17 | FUMBETSU KUDOKU | DISTINCTIONS AND BENEFITS |
| 18 | ZUIKI KUDOKU | THE BENEFITS OF RESPONDING WITH JOY |
| 19 | HOSSHI KUDOKU | BENEFITS OF THE TEACHER OF THE LAW |
| 20 | JO FUKYO BOSATSU | BODHISATTVA NEVER DISPARAGING |
| 21 | NYORAI JINRIKI | SUPERNATURAL POWERS OF THE THUS COME ONE |
| 22 | ZOKURUI | ENTRUSTMENT |
| 23 | YAKUO BOSATSU HONJI | FORMER AFFAIRS OF THE BODHISATTVA MEDICINE KING |

| 24 | MYO'ON BOSATSU | THE BODHISATTVA WONDERFUL SOUND |
|---|---|---|
| 25 | KANZEON BOSATSU FUMON | THE UNIVERSAL GATEWAY OF THE BODHISATTVA PERCEIVER OF THE WORLD'S SOUNDS |
| 26 | DARANI | DHARANI |
| 27 | MYOSHOGON-NO HONJI | FORMER AFFAIRS OF KING WONDERFUL ADORNMENT |
| 28 | FUGEN BOSATSU KAMBOSATSU | ENCOURAGEMENT OF BODHISATTVA UNIVERSAL WORTHY |

## E) PRACTICE

1. <u>Faith, Practice & Study</u>

The three essential aspects which form the basis of Nichiren Buddhism are Faith, Practice & Study. Faith gives rise to Practice & Study and Practice & Study in turn give rise to Faith.

The powers of faith & practice will manifest the power of the Buddha & the Law. The primary practice is chanting Nam Myoho Renge Kyo & carrying out the act of chanting is in itself an act of faith. The twice daily recitation of Gongyo & Daimoku is central to the practice of Nichiren Daishonin's Buddhism. Since Buddhism does not advocate blind faith, a study of its teachings, are an important aspect of deepening our faith & understanding. Sharing with others, one's own experience of developing & expanding their lives, helps to propagate Buddhism.

Nichiren Daishonin's Buddhism is none other than the 'Buddhism of actuality" which attaches importance to practice above all. There is a lasting stable happiness with practice & faith in the Gohonzon & chanting Nam Myoho Renge Kyo – EVERYONE has the potential to experience it. The causes of happiness lie within our own mind.

## FAITH

Faith means to believe in the Gohonzon (Mystic Law) and is itself the manifestation of one's own Buddhahood. Faith enables us to develop a strong spirit which is one with the Mystic law & to tap the limitless power of our inherent Buddhahood.

As Nichiren Daishonin states – "Faith in the sutra means that you will surely attain Buddhahood if you are true to the entirety of the Lotus Sutra, adhering exactly to its teachings without adding any of your own ideas or following the arbitrary interpretations of others." This however does not mean that the teachings or sutras cannot be questioned or that one should have blind belief. As Nichiren Daishonin further states – "… ask any questions you may have about Buddhism. If you do not question and resolve your doubts, you cannot dispel the dark clouds of illusion any more than you can walk a 1000 miles without legs….."

"To accept is easy, to continue is difficult. But Buddhahood lies in continuing faith."

As long as you maintain an indestructible faith, you will never fail to transform adversity into happiness, just like poison changed into water, as described in the "Parable of the skilled physician and his sick children".

Faith in oneself, our abilities and the environment around us, give rise to the myriad different ways in which we go about our day to day lives. In this context, Faith can be likened to trust, which is what it means in Nichiren Buddhism, and leads to the expression that Buddhism equates to daily life. Faith exists only in action and must be coupled with practice & study.

## PRACTICE

Practice means to chant Nam Myoho Renge Kyo, perform gongyo & to teach others the benefits of Buddhism which also brings about one's own Human Revolution. Practice in Nichiren Buddhism falls into two categories – Practice for oneself & practice for others.

The basic practice consists of chanting Nam Myoho Renge Kyo which is supported by the twice daily recitation of gongyo. The practice of gongyo is the recitation of the first part of the Hoben ($2^{nd}$) chapter & the whole of the Juryo ($16^{th}$) chapter followed by the chanting of daimoku. Gongyo is an exercise not just for our bodies, but to purify our minds as a whole It is important that when one chants, we are engaged in a battle to overcome the negative and destructive influences that exist within our lives. The ultimate aim of 'practice for oneself' is to undergo our own human revolution. The ultimate aim of 'practice for others' is kosen rofu, which is to propagate this Buddhism far and wide. Practice for others is based on the profound compassion of "jihi" which is to help others overcome their suffering and gain lasting happiness through the practice of Nichiren Buddhism and is the most pure and noble of all causes.

## STUDY

Study means to understand the Buddhist scriptures (Gosho) and through reason, the differences & points of agreement between this teaching and other systems of thoughts & principles. In Nichiren Buddhism, study means to learn & understand how the principles of Buddhism apply to our daily lives and to use this knowledge to help us attain the supreme happiness of Buddhism. Study is the backbone of faith & practice. Study brings forth immeasurable rewards. We begin to learn to see things with clarity – 'through the eyes of the Buddha' – first by understanding the problems in our lives and then by resolving the same which seemed insurmountable before. As Nichiren Daishonin says – 'When the skies are clear, the ground is illuminated." Without a thorough understanding & comprehension of Nichiren's teachings, one may begin to wrongly interpret true Buddhism. Study will deepen one's understanding & confidence and act as the guiding path towards realizing the ideals of this Buddhism.

Daisaku Ikeda says – "The Philosophy we study must not be one of mere words & ideas. We must all regard this philosophy as alive in the life of each individual."

The four acts of practice - to awaken, reveal, know & enter – is the process undertaken by all people of the nine Worlds to manifest the inherent Buddha wisdom in their lives. 'Awaken' means to firmly believe in the Buddha wisdom inherent in one's life & to have hope for the future. To 'reveal' means to manifest that hope. To 'know' means to be aware of the way to overcome our problems & difficulties faced in our daily lives. To 'enter' means to enter into a state of absolute freedom & happiness.

## 2. Nam Myoho Renge Kyo

The fundamental Law of Life, permeating everything, is Nam Myoho Renge Kyo. It is the expression of the ultimate truth of life. Historically, Myoho-Renge-Kyo is the title & essence of the Lotus Sutra., as translated from Sanskrit into ancient Chinese characters. Nichiren Daishonin placed *nam,* a Sanskrit word meaning 'devotion' in front of these characters. Myoho is the Mystic Law, which exists within the incomprehensible realm of life. Renge means lotus flower, which blooms & seeds at the same time, thus signifying the simultaneity of cause & effect. Kyo literally means sutra, the teachings of Buddha & which encompasses all phenomena in the universe. In simple terms, Nam Myoho Renge Kyo means to devote one's life to the ultimate Law of the universe. Each character contains extremely profound principles of life and together they express how everything in the cosmos works in one harmonious relationship. As president Daisaku Ikeda says: "When we chant Nam Myoho Renge Kyo, with sincere faith in the Gohonzon, even if we don't understand its profound meaning, we can tap the condition of Buddhahood. It is in effect, correctly reading the Lotus Sutra. Our voice chanting Nam Myoho

Renge Kyo, permeates the cosmos and reaches the life condition of Buddhahood and all the Buddhas in the universe. It also penetrates our lives, enabling us to unblock the palace of Buddhahood, or the supreme life condition of eternity, happiness, true self and purity. It is the same as music that, without any explanation, reaches and filters into people's hearts, calling forth a sympathetic response from them."

The invocation, Nam Myoho Renge Kyo, includes within the title the entire Lotus Sutra of eight volumes, twenty eight chapters & 69,384 characters.

As Nichiren Daishonin states, - Myoho Renge Kyo is the king of all sutras, flawless in both letter and principle. This is the reality of life - the Mystic law. Chanting Nam Myoho Renge Kyo will enable one to grasp the mystic truth within you. Even if one neither reads nor studies the Lotus Sutra, chanting the title alone is a source of tremendous good fortune. In a sense chanting Nam Myoho Renge Kyo is probably the most 'user friendly' practice that one is able to encounter.

## NAM

Nam means to devote & dedicate one's self and is known in Japanese as kimyo.

The deepest meaning of Nam encompasses both the action we need to take and the attitude we need to develop if we are to attain Buddhahood in this lifetime. It indicates how we are to practice the Law as revealed in the Lotus Sutra and in terms of Ichinen Sanzen – 3,000 realms in a single moment of existence. As mentioned in the

Gosho – There is little we can gain in terms of elevating our life condition, accumulating benefit and attaining lasting happiness, if our deeds and actions do not match the spirit in which we wish to perform them.

## MYOHO

Myoho means 'mystic law' and expresses the relationship between the life inherent in the universe and the myriad different ways in which this life expresses itself. 'Myo' is the name given to the mystic nature of life and 'ho' to its manifestations. Thus 'myo' refers to the very essence of life, which is unseen, while 'ho' refers to the tangible form that this essence is manifested and apprehended by the senses.

Buddhism adopts a number of interrelated viewpoints to explain the different aspects of 'myoho'.

a. 'Myo' refers to the state of Buddhahood while 'ho' refers to the other nine worlds. 'Myo' refers to our full individual potential while 'ho' refers to that potential we have realized.

b. 'Myo' also refers to death while 'ho' refers to life. Buddhism teaches that the life force immanent in the universe is constantly undergoing a continuous, harmonious rhythm of 'myoho' – that is alternating between the 'unseen' (latent) or 'seen' (manifested) states.

c. In terms of the Three Truths, 'myo' refers to 'ku' (the spiritual aspect - mind) and 'ho' refers to 'ke' (the physical aspect – body)

– the ways that life expresses itself while 'chu' relates to Nam Myoho Renge Kyo, the cadence, oneness and essence of life itself – the Law.
d. In terms of benefits, inconspicuous benefits refers to the unseen world of 'ku' – 'Myo' while conspicuous benefits refers to the manifested world of 'ke' – 'Ho'
e. Myoho is the eternity of life

## RENGE

Renge means Lotus flower. The Lotus flower blooms as an object of beauty amidst a muddy swamp, symbolizing the emergence of our Buddha nature in our everyday lives. The Lotus flower also flowers & seeds at the same time, symbolizing the simultaneity of cause & effect. These concepts form the central tenets of Nichiren Daishonin's Buddhism.

## KYO

Kyo means sutra, the voice or teaching of the Buddha. This may be interpreted as the practice of chanting. Vibrations and waves connect the activity of all phenomena and kyo refers to this activity, indicating that all existence that exists, has existed or will exist is a manifestation of the Mystic Law. Kyo refers to the continuity of life throughout the past, present & future.

## IN A NUTSHELL

The most basic practice of Nichiren Buddhism is to chant Nam Myoho Renge Kyo.
Buddhist teachings state that there is no

difference ultimately between the spiritual & physical aspects of life, the essential reality of life being the same as the multitude of ways in which this life expresses itself. Nam Myoho Renge Kyo, to devote oneself to the Lotus Sutra, does not mean to devote oneself just to the practice of Buddhism, but to life as a whole.

Daisaku Ikeda explains – Nichiren Daishonin, the Buddha of the Latter Day of the Law, embodied the fundamental Law of the universe in the form of a scroll or mandala (Gohonzon). It is our prayers, chanting Nam Myoho Renge Kyo to the Gohonzon, the act of expressing our devotion, which fuses the external cosmos & the inner realm of our minds, enabling one to establish a correct rhythm in the course of our life & daily existence.

Nam Myoho Renge Kyo is the fundamental law for attaining Buddhahood.

Chanting Nam Myoho Renge Kyo manifests Buddhahood in oneself.

Chanting Nam Myoho Renge Kyo enables the pure force of the $9^{th}$ (Buddha) consciousness to purify the $1^{st}$ eight consciousnesses.

Chanting one daimoku is equivalent to one entire reading of the Lotus Sutra.

Chanting daimoku and doing gongyo is akin to conducting a ceremony praising the original Buddha & the great Mystic Law.

### 3. The Three Great Secret Laws

This is the essence of the Buddhist teachings.

The Three Great Secret Laws are Object of Worship (Gohonzon), Daimoku (Invocation of Nam Myoho Renge Kyo) & the High Sanctuary (Place of worship).

The object of worship is the supreme ultimate Buddha of limitless joy from the time of kuon ganjo & is the basis of one's faith & practice. Daimoku is the name of the teaching of this Buddha, a form of practice to the object of worship, and also includes both the aspects of faith & practice. The High Sanctuary signifies the land of this supreme Buddha or places, where the Dai Gohonzon as well as all Gohonzon is enshrined.

These "laws", which form the core of Nichiren Dishonin's Buddhism, are called secret because they transcend the understanding of ordinary people and were only revealed for the first time by Nichiren Daishonin. The three great secret laws constitute the doctrine hidden in the depths of the Juryo (16th) chapter & embody the law which was transferred to Bodhisattva Jogyo, in the Jinriki (21st) chapter for propagation in the latter day.

As stated in the Juryo chapter "I leave this good medicine here for you now. You should take it and not worry that it will not cure you." From Nichiren's viewpoint, "this good medicine" symbolizes the object of worship, the Gohonzon, "Here" symbolizes the place of worship where the Gohonzon is enshrined. "You should take it" signifies that all people should chant Nam Myoho Renge Kyo to the Gohonzon.

What is the significance that can be attached to the Three Great Secret Laws?

Firstly, the object of worship was established in the concrete form of the Gohonzon, which is the basis for the Three Great Secret Laws, as the invocation of Nam Myoho Renge Kyo is directed towards it and the sanctuary is built to enshrine it.

Secondly, chanting Daimoku underlines the importance of one's faith in the Gohonzon, and the strength & depth of this faith is the decisive factor in bringing forth the power of the Gohonzon.

Thirdly, the high sanctuary is the ideal world we seek & which exists in the realities of society and within the realm of our daily living. For our practice, the high sanctuary is our homes, and the place we seek happiness is the world we live in.

### 4. Five Guides for Propagation

These guides are the criteria that Buddhists should take into consideration while propagating the faith.

1. Understanding the scriptures
   This can be fulfilled by dedicated & thorough study of the Buddhism expounded by Nichiren Daishonin.
2. Being aware of the limitations & capacity of the people to understand.
   This can be fulfilled by making sincere

attempts to understand the feelings & backgrounds of the people through dedicated means of communication.

3. Awareness of the current geo-political & socio-economic situation of the environment.

   This can be fulfilled by sharpening ones awareness and timing, so as to arrive at the proper and correct time for propagating the faith when it will be most receptive.

4. An evaluation of society & its culture.

   This can be fulfilled by grasping the manners & customs, patterns of thought & culture of the society in which we are living.

5. A grasp of the philosophies, thoughts & doctrines that have been propagated to the people till that time.

This can be fulfilled by making a close study of the various religions, doctrines & schools of thought that have pervaded & influenced society over the years. After meeting the above criteria we can go about with our genuine efforts for propagating the faith.

### 5. Kosen Rofu

Basically this means to widely declare and spread the teachings. It is the widespread propagation of the Law and its doctrine. The ultimate aim is to awaken the people to the Law & enable them to undergo a profound 'human revolution' & to attain enlightenment (Buddhahood). Improving family life, social & work relationships, is in itself a contributing factor to attainment of kosen – rofu.

Kosen Rofu may be described, in one sense, as the cumulative effect of many people freely undergoing the task of their own 'Human Revolution'. Kosen Rofu includes the practice for others which consist of actions undertaken by one to directly or indirectly lead another to their own eventual enlightenment. This is also known as Shakubuku of which the most basic action is to tell others to chant Nam Myoho Renge Kyo and explain the Buddhist philosophy of life.

Nichiren Daishonin states in poetic terms the effect of Kosen Rofu in society – "The time will come when all people, including those of Learning, Realization & Bodhisattva, will enter on the path to Buddhahood, and the Mystic Law will flourish throughout the land. In that time because all people chant Nam Myoho Renge Kyo together, the wind will not beleaguer the branches or boughs, nor will the rain fall hard enough to break a clod. Disasters will be driven from the land & the people will be rid of misfortune. They will also learn the art of living long, fulfilling lives."

## 6. Supreme Goal of Life

The supreme goal of this practice is to awaken the Buddha nature inherent in everyone's life and to attain Buddhahood.

The preachings of the Lotus Sutra refers to the

concept of "the replacement of the three vehicles (Learning, Realization & Boddhisattva) with the one vehicle (Buddhahood)".

Shakyamuni already proclaimed that the sole purpose of his advent in this world lay in helping all people realize their inherent Buddha nature and to attain Buddhahood. He taught that one had to believe in and live by the Mystic law as indicated in the Lotus Sutra & left a guidepost to enable all people to attain Buddhahood. It was Nichiren Daishonin who clarified the Law as Nam Myoho Renge Kyo. In Buddhist philosophy, the functions of Learning, Realization & Bodhisattva are all indispensable aspects of our lives. Learning enables one to study the Buddhist doctrines, Realization leads one to an understanding of the working of Buddhism in our daily lives, Boddhisattva enables us to act in a compassionate & sympathetic manner towards all people. This leads us to the one Buddha vehicle – Buddhahood.

7. <u>Benefits</u>

a. Embracing & propagating the Mystic Law will minimize or even eradicate the vast accumulation of negative effects of causes created in this lifetime & the infinite past.
b. The powerful way to discover our own Buddha nature is to open ourselves & our faith in the Gohonzon. With continuous practice, we identify with our own

innate wisdom & compassion – our own Buddhahood.

c. Buddhist practice encompasses, both the material & spiritual world & more than that, encourages us to demand actual proof of the validity of our practice.
d. Benefit falls into two categories, conspicuous & inconspicuous. Conspicuous benefits are improvements seen in our environment as a result of our practice. Inconspicuous benefits are increase in energy, inner quality of life, wisdom and the protection afforded by being in rhythm with the Law.
e. In Nichiren Daishonin's Buddhism, "benefit" & "punishment" or gain & loss are the expedient means which leads people to enlightenment.

Nichiren Daishonin explains that there are four different ways in which chanting Nam Myoho Renge Kyo produces benefits.

Conspicuous prayer resulting in conspicuous benefits – this means that by sincerely chanting for what you desire, you quickly achieve it.

Conspicuous prayer resulting in inconspicuous benefits – this means that your desires are fulfilled after a lapse of time. Your inherent Buddha wisdom will make you understand why your desires were not fulfilled at once.

Inconspicuous prayer resulting in conspicuous benefits – this means that a strong and steady practice will build up and accumulate a 'bank' of good fortune and protection.

Inconspicuous prayer resulting in inconspicuous

benefits – this means that a strong and steady practice will over a period of time enable you to attain a realization of your true self, which is Buddhahood. This benefit is also known as 'human revolution'.

## 8. General

### a. Oneness of Person & The Law

According to the teachings of Nichiren Daishonin, the Person & the Law are one. The person is the original Buddha of kuon ganjo & the law is Nam Myoho Renge Kyo, both of which have existed since the infinite past. Because Nichiren realized & manifested the eternal law of Nam Myoho Renge Kyo within himself, he is an embodiment of Nam Myoho Renge Kyo – the Buddha who is one with the law. Thus our goal is to attain the ultimate state of Oneness of the Person & the Law, which is achieved by correctly practicing & following the teachings of Nichiren Daishonin.

The principle of Oneness of Person & Law shows that ordinary people are all potential Buddhas and that although the Law exists externally, Buddhism does not exist apart from human life.

### b. Oneness of Body & Mind / Life & its Environment / Being & Essence

The two aspects of the body (physical) & mind (spiritual) are interrelated phases of the same entity and thus inseparable. Shoho – The realm of living beings. Eho – The realm of the environment.

The principle of Icinen Sanzen clearly states that both shoho & eho are inherent in a single moment of life. Life & its environment are reflections of one another. As Nichiren Daishonin states "Environment is like the shadow and life, its body. Without the body there is no shadow & without life there is no environment. One cannot exist without the other." Esho funi is a principle that shows how people can influence & reform their environment through inner change & the elevation of their life condition. The principle of oneness of life & its environment is based on the unification of the Three Truths – All life has a spiritual, physical & essential aspect & is capable of manifesting the Ten Worlds. The realm of the environment also arises from the single law of life – The Mystic Law.

Buddhism teaches that to blame circumstances for one's misfortunes is shortsighted. One must change that aspect of one's circumstances which has given rise to one's misfortunes and your environment will reflect that change. Essence is integral in the being itself. This idea is represented by the concept of the unification of the three truths (ku, ke, chu). Death is a temporary discontinuance of the functions that make up an individual life, but is not the extinction of life itself. After death, life does not go somewhere else or continue as a 'soul'. Death becomes the merging of the individual & the universe & it extends throughout the universe.

The implication of the Three Truths is that there is no fundamental distinction between the spiritual & physical aspects of life. These are merely two different aspects of our individual life and thus cannot be separated.

We can view our lives as consisting of our thoughts, emotions & demands of our physical bodies, known as our 'inner' life and the universe which we are inextricably linked & which functions to sustain our inner life, and known as our 'outer' life. Just as the environment influences us, so too, we have a profound effect on our environment. As Nichiren Daishonin states – "When the body bends, the shadow bends too". We relate to our environment through our sensory perceptions of our five senses & make judgments based on these perceptions in our sixth sense. In Buddhism this is known as the 'purification' of the six senses. One's body & mind at a single moment pervade the entire realm of phenomena.

One of the fundamental principles of Buddhism is that when the Buddha nature manifests itself from within, it will obtain protection from without.

### c. Chanting / Meditation / Positive Thinking

Meditation serves to centre your thoughts & relax your system. Positive thinking aims to create positive results from a positive state of mind. The practice of chanting Nam Myoho Renge Kyo, is for us to express & experience our own innate Buddhahood & release the powerful energy contained within that (Buddhahood) and change our karma.

When the mind is completely unbound, purely focused & absorbed, it naturally becomes tranquil, clear & lucid.

## F) GENERAL IDEAS, THOUGHTS & TEACHINGS

Our lives, like the universe, undergoes constant change in the cycles of birth (formation), growth & existence (continuance), ageing (decline) and death (disintegration) – merging of life with the universe. This is an eternally continuing cycle of the entity of the Law.

Nichiren Daishonin is the Buddha of the Latter Day of the Law, who inscribed the Dai Gohonzon, which is an embodiment of the Law – Nam Myoho Renge Kyo. His advent was to bring salvation to the people by awakening them to the Law, to enable them to attain enlightenment.

The Human Revolution needed today to change our society, is for each individual to discover the entity of life or Nam Myoho Renge Kyo, within the depths of our lives. This is the ultimate purpose of Kosen Rofu, the propagation of the Law.

As Nichiren Daishonin states – "It is due to the blessings obtained by protecting & embracing the Law that one can diminish, in this lifetime, his suffering & retribution."

The principle of Unity as thought by Nichiren Daishonin, shows us how to unite solidly with unwavering conviction & belief in the universal philosophy which reveals the dignity inherent in all living entities.

We can be identified in the innermost depths of our lives as the original entities of the Mystic Law, who dedicate our lives to propagate the Mystic Law throughout the world. In society we project various images, such as husband, wife, father, mother, teacher, student, clerk, scholar etc. These are continuously changing roles, yet the true entity of life, or the Buddha nature inherent in each of us, is eternal & unchangeable.

Life & Impermanence

Every living thing in the universe is changing, through movement & flow, never staying put in one place. Something that has stopped in one place is not alive. The sun & moon, and even the constellations, are always changing. This earth we depend on, it too is always moving through the universe, alive. The word impermanence does not refer to something that is false, it means 'not continuous' and 'not eternal'. Thus it also means 'not fixed' and 'changing'. This is the true condition of the universe. Life rests within this process of change and through this process of transformation & the mystery of the universe & the exquisite charm of living unfolds. If there was no change, if things were fixed in one place, that would be death, the ceasing of respiration. Through ceaseless change, every single living thing undergoes transformation, again & again. Spring comes & goes and then circulates through summer, fall & winter. This is the breathing, the rhythmic movement of the living universe. So the passage of time is not something to regret. You must master the life wisdom that understands how to use that time well.

Most people have a preconceived fatalistic notion that all human affairs are completely predetermined. Some even criticize the Buddhist concept of causation as fatalistic as if one is bound by karmic forces, how is meaning found in this life. Pre Lotus Sutra teachings state that salvation is only found in the afterlife, by being reborn in the 'Pure Land of Perfect Bliss', and by the grace of a transcendental Buddha to whom one should devote their entire life.

As stated in the Lotus Sutra, Shakyamuni directed us to a source of power that can sever the chains of karmic forces. Nichiren Daishonin identified this entity or Law of Life as Nam Myoho Renge Kyo, as the cause that enables us to sever the chains of Karmic forces & allows new effects to be bought out in the life of every human being. The mere fact that this struggle to overcome karmic forces will result in victory, dispels the feeling of fatalism.

Nam Myoho Renge Kyo is the power that can alter the flow of life.

"Faith in Buddhism is not an abstract concept; separate from day to day reality. Our faith directly affects every aspect of our daily lives, from our belief about ourselves, our relationships with friends and family, to our contribution in society. Through faith, we gain the courage to take action and become experts at living. Those who show care and compassion to others, strive to excel at work and contribute to their communities, show themselves to be people of genuine faith. Without such action, our faith becomes a mere formality."
– Faith in Daily Life.

# G) EXTENDED GLOSSARY

1. <u>Anut Tara Samyak Sambodhi</u>

In Sanskrit, the wisdom of the Buddha is called "Anut Tara Samyak Sambodhi". This means the supreme, perfect & universal wisdom to perceive the Law of the universe.

2. <u>Arhat</u>

This is known in the ancient scriptures as the highest form of enlightenment, achievable by persons of learning, through their Buddhist practice, and as specified in early Hinayana teachings.

3. <u>Bodhisattva</u>

In Sanskrit "Bosatsu" meaning "Awakening Warrior"
Bodhisattva is the expression of total commitment & devotion to aiding & assisting others & indicates a life filled with compassion. A Bodhisattva is one who attains to grasp the Law & attain wisdom, striving for others. Bodhi means wisdom and sattva means a sentient being.
The Lotus Sutra describes the appearance of the bodhisattvas of the Earth, to whom Shakyamuni entrusted the mission of propagating the Lotus Sutra in the Latter Day of the Law. Jogyo is

known as the leader of these Bodhisattvas of the Earth. Nichiren Daishonin appeared in the form of Bodhisattva Jogyo & devoted his entire being to the propagation of the Lotus Sutra –Nam Myoho Renge Kyo & revealed his true identity as the original Buddha of kuon ganjo who made his advent in the Latter Day of the Law.

The Bodhisattvas of theoretical teachings help people by inspiring them with wisdom, courage and other virtues and use their special specific skills to benefit society. They were entrusted by Shakyamuni to propagate his teachings after his death during the two thousand years of the Former & Middle Days of the Law.

The Bodhisattvas of the Earth are disciples of the original true Buddha since time without beginning. They teach and propagate the Mystic law directly. They help people by leading & guiding them to the ultimate Law of Nam Myoho Renge Kyo.

The Bodhisattvas of theoretical teachings are disciples of Shakyamuni in his transient incarnation as a provisional Buddha. These Bodhisattvas help people by inspiring them with wisdom, courage & other virtues. They use their specific skills to benefit society.

4. <u>Buddha Nature</u>

This is an underlying, basic & most subtle nature of mind, completely untainted by negative emotion or thought.

5. <u>Compassion</u>

A state of mind that is non-violent, non-harming & non- aggressive. It is a mental attitude based on the wish for others to be free of their suffering & is associated with a sense of commitment, responsibility & respect towards others.

6. <u>The Concept of Soku</u>

Soku literally means 'the same thing'. However this word has a deeper level of meaning, mainly implying the dynamic idea of transformation. Soku reinforces the view that Buddhahood is not an ethereal or worldly state but a quality expressed in the behavior & practicalities of daily life. Soku implies that there is no distinction between Buddhahood & the other Nine Worlds. Soku is Nam Myoho Renge Kyo. Earnestly chanting Nam Myoho Renge Kyo brings about an inner transformation in our activities.

7. <u>Dharma</u>

Dharma is the doctrine of Buddha's teachings. It is the true nature of phenomena. (Sanskrit – To hold (back) from the suffering)

## 8. The Entity of Life

Nichiren Daishonin's Buddhism teaches that the 'life entity' has existed since 'time without beginning'. This entity appears as a result of the combined effects of the various causes contained within it from the infinite past and when meeting with the correct conditions at that precise moment. This life entity continues unaltered during the individual's life span, disappears at death but remains unaltered in nature, to reappear in the future in a different form depending upon the causes and conditions prevailing at that time.

Buddhism denies the existence of the soul and teaches instead what is known as the 'non substantiality of persons (ku)'. An individual is merely a temporary fusion of the Five Components which arise as a result of particular causes and conditions prevailing at that moment, and has no fixed identity or absolute self that exists throughout eternity.

## 9. Eye Opening Ceremony

This ceremony is conducted when a new Gohonzon is enshrined.

## 10. Fivefold Comparison

These are the five successive levels of comparison set forth by Nichiren Daishonin to demonstrate the superiority of Nam Myoho Renge Kyo over all other Buddhist teachings. They are 1. Buddhism vs Non Buddhist teachings 2. Mahayana Buddhism vs Hinayana Buddhism 3. True Mahayana vs Provisonal Mahayana 4. The Essential Teachings of the Lotus Sutra vs the Theoretical Teachings of the Lotus Sutra 5. The Buddhism of Sowing vs the Buddhism of Harvest.

## 11. The Five Components

Each individual life form is the temporary fusion of the Five Components – Form, perception, conception, volition & consciousness. A life form appears when the Five Components come together within the life entity and as a result of past causes and present effects & conditions – and disappears when they disunite.

'Form' is indicated by the body which contains the five sense organs through which one perceives and assimilates information regarding the environment. 'Perception' is the act of receiving this data through the five sense organs and integrating it in the sixth sense organ - the mind. 'Conception' is the ability to form a judgment based on the perceived data. "Volition' is the ability to take action based on the data received and perceived. 'Consciousness" is the act to discern things in both, the abstract & materialistic sense, to make judgments and to take action.

Together the Five Components constitute the essential elements of an individual life.

## 12. The Five Skandas

These are the:
Suffering of birth
Suffering of decay
Suffering of illness
Suffering of losing things close to us
Suffering of death

## 13. The Four Noble Truths / Paths

These are - Root of sufferings, Cause of sufferings, Way out of sufferings, Cultivation of Dharma. These are more commonly characterized as the four higher worlds – Learning, Realization, Bodhisattva & Buddhahood.

## 14. The Fourteen Slanders

The Fourteen Slanders are listed as – Arrogance, Negligence, Arbitrary/egotistical judgment, Shallow/self satisfied understanding, Attachments to earthly desires, Lack of seeking spirit, Not believing in the Buddha's teachings, Aversion, Deluded doubt, Vilification, Contempt, Hatred, Jealousy & grudges and Comments. The Fourteen Slanders undermine any action we may take to create value. For example, there is a difference if one was to invocate daimoku, chanting Nam Myoho Renge Kyo, while acting against the intent of the Lotus Sutra. In order to manifest our single minded yearning to see our Buddha nature, we must not begrudge our lives.

## 15. The Eightfold Noble Paths

The Eightfold Noble Paths are the eight principles governing one's behaviour. Right views (knowledge), right thinking (thoughts), right speech, right action, right way of life (livelihood), right endeavor (effort), right mindfulness (attentiveness) and right meditation (concentration).

The Eightfold Noble Paths was one of the first and best known teachings of Shakyamuni. A true and honest reflection of our "Right" state of mind will open up the purest part of our soul – our innate Buddha Nature

## 16. Gohonzon

The Gohonzon is the object of worship in Nichiren Daishonin's Buddhism. It is the transcription of the Dai-Gohonzon (Dai meaning great), inscribed by Nichiren Daishonin, on a paper scroll. Down the centre in large characters are the words 'Nam Myoho Renge Kyo – Nichiren ', representing the Oneness of the Person & the Law. Grouped around are smaller Chinese & Sanskrit characters, which represent the totality of life itself. Nichiren Daishonin was inherently enlightened to the Law & realized it himself. The Gohonzon embodies the enlightened life condition of Nichiren Daishonin & represents life in its highest possible state – Buddhahood. Having sincere faith and chanting to the Gohonzon leads the way for everyone to attain the supreme life condition of Buddhahood.

Go means 'worthy of honor' and honzon means 'object of fundamental worship'. Together they signify that the Gohonzon is the true object of worship. It is so called because it is able to give happiness to all people. However it is important to note that the Gohonzon is not a deity or external force which has transcendental powers, but an object which draws, from deep within us, our inherent Buddha nature. As Nichiren Daishonin says – "Never seek this Gohonzon outside yourself. The Gohonzon exists only within the mortal flesh of us ordinary people who embrace the Lotus Sutra & chant Nam Myoho Renge Kyo."

Another phrase used by Nichiren Daishonin to describe the Gohonzon is 'kanjin no honzon' which means the object for observing one's mind & finding the Ten Worlds within it. The Gohonzon is like a mirror that enables us to see our lives clearly in terns of our Buddha nature.

Chanting to the Gohonzon is akin to conducting our own 'Ceremony in the Air' and leads to a fusion of the Law, which exists within our lives and the universe. As Nichiren Daishonin says – "The Gohonzon is the object of worship which perfectly depicts Shakyamuni in the Treasure Tower and all the other Buddhas who were present, as accurately as the print matches the woodblock." Continuously chanting Nam Myoho Renge Kyo leads to the fusion of our lives with the Gohonzon, thus opening the way for people to attain happiness & enlightenment in their own lifetimes.

The Dai Gohonzon is not the only and foremost object of worship. All Gohonzon are equally the object of worship.

As Nikko Shonin, the 26th high priest of Nichiren Shoshu states – "The Dai Gohonzon is the origin of all Buddhas and the place to which they all return. The blessings of all the Buddhas and sutras throughout space & time all return to the Gohonzon which provides the seed of Buddhahood and is hidden in the Lotus Sutra. This Gohonzon provides great & boundless benefits. Its mystic functions are vast & profound. If you take faith in this Gohonzon, even for a short while, no prayer will go unanswered, no sin will remain unforgiven, all good fortune will be bestowed, and all righteousness will be proven."

17. <u>Gosho</u>

The Gosho is a collection of text & writings which contain the teachings of Nichiren Daishonin.

'Go' means worthy of great respect while 'Sho' means writings. Part of the Gosho consists of letters from Nichiren Daishonin to his followers, while the other part consists of formal doctrinal treatises aimed at a more learned audience such as scholars and the religious & secular authorities of that time. A study of these writings, play an important and vital role in Nichiren Buddhism.

## 18. The High Sanctuary

The Japanese word for sanctuary is 'kaidan'. Kai - meaning precepts, and dan - meaning a dais used for ordination. In other words, a sanctuary where vows are taken in a ceremony. In Nichiren Buddhism, the place where one chants daimoku to the Gohonzon is termed as the High Sanctuary. The Dai Gohonzon –the object of worship – is enshrined in the Sho-Hondo, the High Sanctuary – at Taiseki-ji. The places where other Gohonzon are enshrined can also be termed as sanctuaries.

## 19. Human Revolution

The change deep in oneself, in the way we perceive life, society & the world. It is an unwavering & absolute conviction in the eternity of life. It is a process by which an individual gradually expands his life, conquers his negative and destructive tendencies, and ultimately makes the state of Buddhahood his dominant life condition. Human Revolution is both the process & the goal of our Buddhist practice.

Human Revolution means the reformation of one's life & way of living. We can achieve this reformation by establishing a powerful, independent self in the depths of our life, which brings forth value from every situation we face.

The Human Revolution of discovering the entity of Nam Myoho Renge Kyo, within our beings, will fill us with life force & wisdom to enable us to succeed & overcome any situation.

## 20. Impermanence

It characterizes everything in the Universe. It is a law which states that all conditioned things arise & disappear. Nothing is constant. Observing all phenomena from this angle is an essential feature of Buddhism.

## 21. Jigage

A verse form of teaching.

## 22. Kuon Ganjo

Kuon means infinite past & ganjo means the beginning of all things. The concept of Kuon Ganjo does not mean just infinite past, but indicates a time without beginning, an eternity, with no beginning or end, beyond the confines of time. In this sense, eternity is the unbroken continuance of a single moment. Thus the present moment contains the ultimate existence in which the past without beginning & the infinite future are both contained. Kuon Ganjo thus encompasses the present moment.

## 23. Life & Death

One of the issues of greatest importance and eternal relevance is how we face death, the inescapable destiny of all living beings. For in the face of death, external factors such as social status or position count for naught. Everything depends on one's faith, one's state of life. It is our attitude to death that fundamentally affects our whole attitude to life.

In today's age with increasing levels of logic & reasoning, scientific proof is demanded for all things. Skeptics will say that because of a lack of clear evidence in the after life – no such thing happens. Therefore all religions or beliefs that advocate an after life – Christianity & Islam teach about eternal life in Heaven or Hell, Buddhism & other Eastern beliefs teach about periodic reincarnations – are attempts to placate people and instill the consoling idea of future benefits or punishment based on present sufferings or wrong doings.

When most people talk of Buddhism, the thought that springs to mind is reincarnation with its attendant connotations as being reborn as insects or plant life as punishment for the sins committed in previous lifetimes.

Nichiren Daishonin considered reaching an understanding of death as his greatest challenge. He states: "Ever since my childhood, I have studied Buddhism with one thought in mind. Life is pathetically fleeting. Nothing suffices to describe this transience. No one can escape death. My sole wish has therefore been to solve this eternal mystery. All else has been secondary."

Buddhism regards life & death as merely two different phases experienced by the same entity of life. Sleep, like death is a fundamental and mysterious aspect of life. Both sleep and death express the continual rhythm and energy of myoho, the Mystic Law. As Chuang – Tzu, a Chinese Taoist said in the 3rd century BC 'everything is one: during sleep (death) the soul, undistracted, is absorbed into this unity: when awake (alive), distracted, it sees the different beings "

## 24. Note on the Parable of the Skilled Physician & his Sick Children

There was once a physician who was skilled in compounding medicines & curing all kinds of ailments. He had many children. He traveled to distant lands to cure people. During one of his travels, his children mistakenly drink some poison and fall sick. The physician returns and the children, even though they are very sick, are overjoyed to see him and beg for him to cure them. The father gathers various herbs & prepares a prescription of the finest flavor, color & fragrance. He gives a dose of this concoction to his children, telling them that it is a highly effective medicine & taking it will cause them to be relieved of their suffering & illness. Those children, who are not so sick, see that the medicine is good and take it immediately, and are cured of their sickness. The children who are very sick, though happy to see their father return and having begged him to cure them, refuse to take the medicine. Their minds are too sick to comprehend the benefit of the medicine. The physician/father, seeing this, understands that their minds are too befuddled. He decides to resort to 'expedient means' to make them take the medicine. He tells them that he is old & close to death. He departs for another land and leaves the medicine for them to take and assures them of its curative properties. He then sends back a messenger to tell his children that he has died. When the children hear of his 'death', they are filled with grief, consternation & self pity. At last they come to their senses, realize the benefit of the medicine & take it, thus causing them to be cured of their illness. On hearing that his children have been cured, the physician/father returns.

Do his actions deem that the father was guilty of lying???????

IMPLICIT MEANING
The physician is Shakyamuni who attained enlightenment in the distant past. The children represent the all the people. Shakyamuni understands the sufferings of the people. He imparts the wisdom of the Lotus Suitra to them. In Nichiren Buddhism, the Gohonzon is the ultimate medicine. Those who embrace Nam Myoho Renge Kyo, will have their sufferings quickly relieved & realize a blissful life. Some of the people are in a state of hell & it is difficult

for them to understand the benefit of the Mystic Law. The Buddha, through various bodhisattvas, spread the Mystic Law in the Latter Day after his 'extinction' (kosen-rofu). The spread of the Mystic law is achieved through propagation of the Lotus Sutra and teachings left behind by Shakyamuni after his 'extinction'. The Mystic Law enables each person to realize they are originally a Buddha in their own right.

## 25. Principal of Causality

This is commonly known as the relationship between cause and effect. Every manifestation has a cause.
Simply put – the best method of ensuring that a certain type of event does not take place is to make sure that the causal conditions that normally give rise to that event, no longer arise. Conversely, if you want something to happen, accumulate the causes and conditions that give rise to it. If one makes good causes one will receive like positive effects. If one makes bad causes one will receive like negative effects.
Pre Lotus Sutra teachings expound the Law of Causality as effects of causes made in past lifetimes which manifest themselves in the present and subsequent future lifetimes and thus affecting our lives for countless kalpas. This teaching has no relevance in this Latter Day of the Law. A teaching is required that will enable us to break through the shackles of the principle of causality of the pre Lotus Sutra teachings and

to tap into our inherent Buddha nature. It was Nichiren Daishonin who established the Law as outlined in the Lotus Sutra and as expounded by Shakyamuni. This enables ordinary people in their daily lives to break through their past causes and effects, by devoting their lives to the Mystic Law – chanting Nam Myoho Renge Kyo, and return as their enlightened true selves as they were in the distant past of time without beginning.

Daisaku Ikeda says – "Nichiren Daishonin's Buddhism, based on the principle of simultaneity of cause & effect teaches that we can change our karma and, further, that by doing so we can also change society."

26. <u>Rebirth</u>

The process of rebirth may be compared to the succession of one wave form in the ocean by another, where, though the substance of one does not pass into the other, yet is wholly dependant on the nature of the former – each wave form representing a life as we commonly term it.

27. <u>Rissho Ankoku Ron</u>

It is said that the Buddhism of Nichiren Daishonin begins and ends with "Rissho Ankoku Ron" – a timeless document which discusses the effect of people's beliefs on society and their environment, applicable through time & age. The English translation is "Treatises on securing the peace of the land through the propagation of true Buddhism".

## 28. Samsara

This is also known as the ocean of mortality. It is a state of existence characterized by endless cycles of Life, Death & Rebirth. All beings remain in this state, propelled by karmic imprints from past actions & negative delusory states of mind, until one removes all negative tendencies of mind & achieves a state of liberation.

## 29. The Six Paramitas

In Sanskrit, 'paramita' means having reached the opposite shore. In Buddhism, this shore means the world of the common mortal while the opposite shore is that of an enlightened one. Bodhisattva practices are likened to the crossing to the shore of enlightenment. The process of 'reaching', the other shore entails the practice of the six paramitas, practices that must be carried out in order to reach enlightenment.

The Six Paramitas consist of Charity, Keeping the commandments, Patience under insult, Zeal, Progress meditation, Wisdom (The power to discern reality).

Charity means giving relief & preaching the Law. Keeping the commandments means observing the precepts and practicing the correct modes of behavior and living. Patience means forbearance under hardship & opposition. Zeal means to assiduously carry out the practices as set forth. Progress meditation means to focus and contemplate the eternal truth with an open mind. Wisdom means to perceive the true nature of all things and correctly recognize the eternal truth.

However the Lotus Sutra reveals that by embracing the Mystic Law, one does not have to practice the six paramitas to attain enlightenment but will be naturally endowed with their benefits. The Buddha is a supreme being, completely endowed with all these requirements.

## 30. Soka Kyoiki Gakkai

This association was founded by Tsunesaburo Makiguchi & Josei Toda in 1930. It gradually developed into an organization dedicated to promoting the practice & spread of Nichiren Buddhism. During WWII, the Japanese authorities cracked down on the organization in an effort to strengthen the ideological control on the masses. Twenty one leaders of the SKG were arrested in 1943. Only Makiguchi & Toda refused to compromise their beliefs. Makiguchi died in prison in 1944. Josei Toda was released in July 1945 and dedicated the rest of his life reconstructing the organization which he renamed the Soka Gakkai (Value Creating Society).

## 31. Three Aspects of Life

The concept of the three aspects of life is closely related to the three truths and the three virtues. The three aspects of life are:
   a. Physical aspect (Ojin) - Property of Action (Temporary existence of the three truths).
   b. Spiritual aspect (Hoshin) - Property of Wisdom
   c. Aspect of essence (Hosshin) - Property of the Law (The Middle Way)

A Buddha is invariably endowed with all three properties. The Buddha is not a theoretical entity, in essence, (Hosshin), but a person with compassionate action, (Ojin), & profound wisdom, (Hoshin) – an enlightened human being.

## 32. The Three Calamities & Seven Disasters

The Three Calamities are High grain prices (inflation), Warfare & Pestilence.
The Seven Disasters are Sickness & plague, Invasion from foreign lands, Internal revolution, Aberrations in the solar system, Solar & lunar eclipses, Unseasonable weather, and Severe droughts.
It is said that when the true teachings of Buddhism are obscured & disregarded, it leads to the life force of the people being sapped leading to apathy and resignation to their fate (cause),

which in turn leads to the appearance of The Three Calamities & Seven Disasters, which must ensue (effect)

The Three Calamities & Seven Disasters are the result of disharmony in the realms of nature, human society and the self.

The sutras teach that the basic causes of the Three Calamities are human desire & greed, in the case of inflation; anger, in the case of warfare; and stupidity, in the case of pestilence. The concept of the Three Calamities is therefore clearly inseparable from the Three Poisons inherent in life – Greed, Anger and Stupidity.

## 33. The Three Enlightened Bodies

The Dharma Body – This is the Mystic Law, the eternal truth.

The Bliss Body – This is the wisdom to awaken to this Law.

The Manifested Body – This is the enactment of the Law to lead and guide people to enlightenment.

## 34. The Three Obstacles & Four Devils

Nichiren Daishonin referred to the three obstacles and the four devils in WND 501. In general this represent the negative forces prevalent in all life that tend to diminish the value of our lives, cause disharmony and undermine our self reliance, and which ultimately obstruct and test the progress of our Buddhist faith and practice.

The three obstacles are:

a) Eartly desires arising from the three poisons -Greed, Anger & Stupidity
b) Karma
c) Retribution – Obstruction from outside forces in practicing our Buddhist faith.

The four devils are:
a) The Five Components – Hardship caused by our physical or mental states.
b) Earthly desires – That which negatively affects the mind.
c) Death – Cessation of our practice.
d) Devil of the 6$^{th}$ heaven – Fundamental negativity inherent in our lives.

## 35. The Three Vehicles

The three vehicles of the Buddhist faith are Learning, Realization & Bodhisattva (Learning, Meditation & Wisdom). The Hinayana philosophies led people to seek the first two vehicles & those who achieved these states were led to believe that they could enter Nirvana by eradicating all desires. Shakyamuni however encouraged his disciples to become bodhisattvas & help others. This is consistent with earlier Mahayana teachings. Both streams of Buddhism however share the same major feature that Buddhahood was attainable after practicing austerities over many lifetimes.

It was only after the Lotus Sutra was expounded that Shakyamuni stated that all people could attain Buddhahood in this lifetime by believing & living by the Mystic Law, thus replacing the

Three Vehicles with the One Supreme Vehicle – Buddhahood.

However, the Buddhist philosophy regards the functions of Learning, Realization & Bodhisattva as indispensable aspects of our lives, because they are not ends in themselves, but a means to lead us to the one Buddha vehicle.

The teachings of the Buddha prior to the Lotus Sutra, expounded the Three Paths or 'Three Vehicles' which lead to Buddhahood. These are teachings that are explicitly expounded to suit the capacity of Voice Bearers (world of learning), Cause Awakened Ones (world of realization) & Bodhisattvas. However the Lotus Sutra makes clear that the doctrine of the 'Three Vehicles' does not reveal the true intent of the Buddha, which is to reveal a single path that leads all people to Buddhahood. This is known as the 'replacement of the three vehicles with the one vehicle'. Only the Lotus Sutra constitutes the one Buddha vehicle. The sutra clarifies that Shakyamuni expounded the 'Three Vehicles' as an expedient means for illuminating the one Buddha vehicle.

## 36. The Thirty Four Negatives

From the Chinese translations of the sutras, the text reads as:

"The entity is neither existence nor non existence; neither cause nor circumstance; neither itself nor another; neither square nor round; neither short nor long; neither rising nor falling; neither birth

nor death; neither creation nor appearance, nor artificial; neither sitting nor lying; neither going nor staying; neither moving nor rolling, nor still; neither advancing nor retreating; neither safe nor in danger; neither reasonable nor unreasonable; neither gain nor loss; neither this nor that; neither past nor future; neither blue, nor yellow, nor red nor white; neither scarlet nor purple nor any other color;"
In Chinese grammar this passage is expressed with a total of thirty four negatives.

## 37. True & Provisional Buddhas,

The Buddha appears in this world in order to lead the people to the supreme vehicle of Buddhahood. In the Latter Day of the Law, Nichiren Daishonin clarified the Buddha wisdom, the ultimate truth as Nam Myoho Renge Kyo – the universal Law.
The true identity of the Buddha and the temporary aspects he assumes can be compared, respectively, to the moon shining in the sky & its reflection on the surface of a pond. The former is called the true Buddha and the latter are called provisional Buddhas. The teachings expounded by the true Buddha are called hommon or essential teachings & those expounded by a provisional Buddha, shakumon or theoretical teachings.
As long as Shakyamuni said he was enlightened in his present incarnation, he was a provisional Buddha, but when he revealed his original

enlightenment, in the distant past, he was acting as the true Buddha.

Nichiren Buddha is identified as the original Buddha who has been enlightened to the ultimate truth in the infinite past. He clarified the cause for Shakyamuni's enlightenment as the ultimate Law of Nam Myoho Renge Kyo.

Therefore the theory of Shakyamuni's enlightenment still does not explain the Buddha's true entity in its entirety. This is why, from the standpoint of Nichiren Buddhism, even Shakyamuni is called a provisional Buddha, and Nichiren Daishonin, the manifestation of the original Buddha from kuon ganjo, is called the true Buddha who appeared as the Buddha of the Latter Day of the Law.

## 38. Yuga / Kalpa

A word derived from ancient Indian cosmology which means an extremely long period of time.

# **CONCLUSION**

**Nichiren Daishonin's words to his followers:**

"Therefore I say to you, my disciples, try practicing as the Lotus Sutra teaches, exerting yourselves without begrudging your lives! Test the truth of Buddhism! Nam Myoho Renge Kyo! Nam Myoho Renge Kyo! Nam Myoho Renge Kyo!"

# **ACKNOWLEDGEMENTS**

My faith has enabled me to complete this book, which I vowed I would write one day, albeit this vow was made in more trying times and under desperate circumstances. As Henry W Longfellow stated: "Great is the art of beginning, but greater is the art of ending."

In particular I would like to offer my heartfelt gratitude:

To my wife, Raju, for her unstinting faith and belief and above all, for introducing me to the amazing world of Nichiren Buddhism.

To the writings of Nichiren Daishonin from where I have been able to draw strength, conviction and courage to complete this book.

To President Daisaku Ikeda, for his vision and writings which truly guided me in the writing of this book.

To our wonderful family of the HKSGI HQ 10, without whose love, prayers and support, our lives would have been vastly different.

To Angie Robinson for her guidance, support and the numerous reading materials I had ingress to, and above all, for being a wonderful and caring friend.

To all the various authors of books, publications, magazines and various reading material from whom I have been draw upon and truly able to understand and appreciate the philosophy of Nichiren Buddhism.

Lightning Source UK Ltd.
Milton Keynes UK
UKHW041415011021
391502UK00001B/112